GEM STONES A TO Z

OTHER BOOKS BY DIANE STEIN

A Woman's I Ching
All Women Are Healers
All Women Are Psychics
Casting the Circle
Diane Stein's Guide to Goddess Craft
Essential Energy Balancing
Essential Energy Balancing II
Essential Energy Balancing III
Essential Psychic Healing
Essential Reiki
Essential Reiki Teaching Manuel
Healing with Gemstones and Crystals
Healing with Flower and Gemstone Essences
The Holistic Puppy
Lady Sun, Lady Moon
Natural Healing for Dogs and Cats
The Natural Remedy Book for Dogs and Cats
The Natural Remedy Book for Women
On Grief and Dying
Pendulums and the Light
Prophetic Visions of the Future
Reliance on the Light
We Are the Angels
The Woman's Book of Healing

Diane Stein on DVD

○

Diane Stein's Essential Reiki Workshop

Visit Diane Stein's website at www.dianestein.net for books, jewelry, workshops, and more.

A HANDY REFERENCE TO HEALING CRYSTALS

GEMSTONES A TO Z

Diane Stein

CROSSING PRESS
Berkeley | Toronto

For Brede and Jeshua

Healing and medicine are two different fields, and the law requires this disclaimer. The information in this book is metaphysical rather than medical and does not constitute medical advice. In case of illness, consult the professional of your choice.

Crossing Press
A division of Ten Speed Press
PO Box 7123
Berkeley CA 94707
www.tenspeed.com

Distributed in Australia by Simon and Schuster Australia, in Canada by Ten Speed Press Canada, in New Zealand by Southern Publishers Group, in South Africa by Real Books, and in the United Kingdom and Europe by Publishers Group UK.

Cover and text design by The Book Designers
Illustrations by Ian Everard
Cover and interior photography by The Book Designers
Gemstone specimens courtesy of
F. Joseph Smith's Massage Therapy Center
158 Almonte Boulevard, Mill Valley, CA 94941

Library of Congress Cataloging-in-Publication Data
Stein, Diane, 1948–
Gemstones A to Z : a handy reference to healing crystals / Diane Stein.
p. cm.
Includes index.
ISBN 1-58091-187-0 (978-1-58091-187-0 : alk. paper)
1. Precious stones—Therapeutic use. 2. Gems—Therapeutic use.
3. Crystals—Therapeutic use. I. Title.
RZ560.S74 2007
615.8'56—dc22
2007032401

First printing, 2008
Printed in Canada
1 2 3 4 5 6 7 8 9 10 — 12 11 10 09 08

CONTENTS

INTRODUCTION ◦ *vi*
A Rainbow of Rocks and Colors
The Confusion of Gemstones Today
Choosing Gemstones for Healing
Dedicating and Clearing Gemstones
Understanding the Kundalini and Hara Line Chakras
Using This Book
Illustrations
The Kundalini Chakras
The Hara Line Chakras
Glossary of Terms

GEMSTONES LISTINGS ◦ *1*

INDEX OF STONES ◦ *235*

INTRODUCTION

A RAINBOW OF ROCKS AND COLORS

When I first discovered gemstones and crystals for healing and metaphysics, there was very little to choose from. Working with gemstones primarily meant using clear quartz crystals, always from Arkansas and usually small, rough, unpolished quartz points of an inch or two in size. Colored gemstones included only a few basic choices such as amethyst and rose quartz. A few healers who had great interest in gemstones knew how to use smoky quartz, blue sodalite and lapis, green aventurine, and peach carnelian—but not much else. In the late 1970s and early 1980s, there wasn't much else available.

Gemstones and crystals were hard to find at that time. Most of my first stones were tumbled pieces, about an inch long, and came from a museum gift shop; there were no metaphysical stores then. A few came from lapidary stores that only sold raw specimens in varying sizes, which were unappealing and usually dirt-covered chunks often at very high prices. Some gemstones came from old jewelry, usually beads and an occasional pendant. The rest came from the women's music festivals that were just beginning to happen, where raw stones, tumbled stones, gemstone jewelry, and sometimes even gemstone pendulums were available and much sought after.

Things are much changed today. Gemstones and crystals are available in a great many types and colors that were unknown twenty-five years ago, and they come from sources worldwide. They can be bought from metaphysical shops, nature stores, jewelry stores, gift shops of all kinds, pagan sources, department stores, lapidaries, gem and mineral shows, bead shows and stores, commercial and designer jewelers, on the Internet including eBay, and a variety of other outlets. Stones may be ordered online directly from crystal and gemstone mines worldwide, and sometimes by visiting the mines. Gemstones and crystals are found in every kind of jewelry and come as specimens, beads, raw pieces and points, polished and cut points and shapes, gemstone skulls, carvings, chips, wands and obelisks, eggs and spheres, cabochons, faceted jewelry shapes, sacred geometry sets, hearts, and animal and Goddess statues—to list just some of the possibilities.

Gemstones and crystals arrive in the United States from all over the world. Hong Kong is the central clearinghouse for gemstone beads, with India a close second. Brazil is a primary source for such stones as amethyst, rose quartz, smoky quartz, the tourmalines, aquamarine, and clear quartz crystal. Moonstone and many of the rarer specimens and precious stones (rubies, sapphires, and emeralds) come from India. China has become a major player in mining and selling fluorite, turquoise, jade, and gemstone carvings, as well as other stones for which Hong Kong is a clearing center. Poland and various former Soviet Union countries offer amber, moldavite, and zincite. Africa provides malachite and many varieties of jasper. Australia offers opals and prehnite. And these are just a few.

The high prices of gemstones twenty-five years ago limited most healers to using tumbled stones, crystal points smaller than three inches, raw chunks, and a few less expensive lapidary specimens but this is no longer the case. Tumbled stones are still inexpensive—several for a dollar—even cheaper now than they used to be, and many more gemstone forms are available and affordable. Many women prefer jewelry and beads including gemstone chip necklaces that cost only a couple of dollars, striking gemstone jewelry and bead strands at a wide variety of prices. Gemstone spheres now start at less than twenty dollars, and less than ten dollars for small ones. Small carvings can cost even less. Crystal skulls remain high priced but are more available, and many people are drawn to working with them. Small quartz points can cost as little as a dollar apiece and affordable larger specimens of all sizes are common. Stones that once seemed totally unattainable are now affordable, even precious stones like natural opals, rubies, sapphires, and emeralds in raw pieces, cabochons, beads, or tumbled form. Shopping around to find the best price is always a good idea. The variety is endless and gemstones and crystals are more available and affordable today than ever before.

THE CONFUSION OF GEMSTONES TODAY

Along with availability, however, come inevitable problems. Not all merchants are honest or even knowledgeable about what they are selling. Commercial names may not reflect what a stone really is. The large and beautiful variety of jasper types that has appeared in the last several years is a case in point. Each type of jasper has a name, but sellers don't always use the same name for the same type of stone. Ocean jasper can mean a stone with a variety of mixed colors in it, usually green, brown, dark red, and grey. The same name can also be given to a type of jasper that is black with swirls of white through it, or one that is brown, grey, cream, and black. Picture jasper is the name for a jasper type that is usually caramel brown with darker hair-like inclusions—or for a stone that is brown with grey and moss green in interesting landscape patterns. Fancy jasper may be the name for the mixed colors of ocean jasper, or it may refer to red and green bloodstone. It can also be a generic name given to any jasper variety by confused sellers. A jasper that is grey, black, and light brown is called Picasso stone, but it can be mislabeled as any of the other jasper names. Chrysocolla jasper is a dyed form of jasper; it is not chrysocolla. With so much confusion, it is necessary to view a stone before buying it to know what you're getting, and even then you may only be sure that it's jasper, not which type.

Likewise a stone I know as Chinese writing rock, a darker caramel brown stone with inclusions and line markings of orange or gold, is called golden lace agate by some sources. African jade is not jade, but is another form of jasper, as is yellow turquoise, which is not turquoise at all. New jade is not jade but serpentine, though higher quality serpentine jade does have healing properties similar to those of traditional jade (which is nearly extinct and therefore much harder to find and more expensive).

Some of this may be attributed to confusion about definitions of similar stones, but other examples are plain dishonesty. When man-made, lab-created, or synthetic stones are not plainly identified, it can only be dishonesty. Hemalyke is an example of a synthetic material often confused for the natural gemstone hematite. Magnetic hematite is also synthetic; the natural form is not magnetized. Swarovski crystal is not natural quartz crystal but is man-made lead crystal. It can be easily distinguished from natural quartz crystal as it glitters in rainbow colors where natural quartz does not. Cinnabar is red lacquered wood, or machine-carved layered lacquer. It is sometimes added to reconstituted (heat melted) quartz and called cinnabar quartz. Goldstone and blue goldstone are ceramic materials and are not natural gemstones. Larimar, a lovely and increasingly rare gemstone from the Dominican Republic, is found only in light robin's egg blue, sometimes with reddish inclusions. Pink larimar is not real larimar but is made from pink conch shells.

Some turquoise is not natural turquoise but dyed howlite, a white stone that absorbs dye colors easily. Turquoise, by the way, is usually stabilized with plastic since turquoise is soft and crumbles easily when used in jewelry. (As previously mentioned, yellow turquoise is a variety of jasper.)

Another of the more egregious of these deceptions is the recent appearance of rainbow moonstone in a variety of garish primary colors. Rainbow moonstone is mottled clear and white, and it is actually white labradorite rather than moonstone. It is being sold today in a variety of dye treatments—purple or amethyst rainbow moonstone, sapphire rainbow moonstone, ruby rainbow moonstone, red onyx rainbow moonstone, and aqua rainbow moonstone. The blue rainbow moonstone found in jewelry pendants is created by placing a piece of black electrical type between the setting and the stone. The natural stone does not come in any of these colors.

Be wary of stones that are dyed glass, dyed quartz crystal or even plastic, usually dyed to bright unnatural colors. These can include cherry quartz, pineapple quartz, and some of the colors of serpentine, or new, jade. If a gemstone's color is improbable, it is likely not a natural stone. If you suspect that the material is glass or plastic, look closely for seams or bubbles in it. Natural gemstones do not have either. "Reconstituted" means that gemstone scraps have been heated until they melt together, sometimes with plastic added as a binder, and then molded. Reconstituted quartz with cinnabar, called cinnabar quartz, is an example of this. A less suspect example is copal amber, which is melted amber formed into beads or often used as incense. Amber is soft, and it is a resin rather than a stone, though it is generally known as a gemstone, and copal is considered an honest use of it.

Some precious stones today are being grown in laboratories, and they are called lab-created gemstones. Most of the sapphires and faceted rubies and many commercial opals with "fire" are created in labs. So are such stones as alexandrite (which is extremely rare and expensive as a natural stone) and Siberian quartz. Whether to consider these stones or any of the other previously mentioned variations—except those that are synthetic, glass or plastic—as valid for healing is very much up to the individual user. Lab-created stones are beautiful, and they definitely have energy. Misnamed stones are still gemstones with valid healing properties. Unnaturally dyed stones, in my opinion, have been artificially altered and are less effective for healing. Synthetic and reconstituted materials are worthless, as are glass and plastic; they are not gemstones.

Also be aware of natural gemstones that have been altered or changed in other ways. If your smoky quartz specimen is shiny but completely and deeply black, it is quartz crystal that has been turned black by irradiation. The life force in the stone is probably dead, certainly wounded, and not a good energy for healing work. Natural smoky quartz is not black; when held up to the light it is a translucent, beer-bottle brown. The only natural smoky quartz that is truly black is from Colorado and has a rough matt finish, rather than the shiny glassy finish of irradiated quartz crystal. Citrine may be altered amethyst, heat-treated to turn the color from purple to yellow. Most heat treated citrine is an orange color, while natural citrine (from Brazil or Scotland usually) is a very pale shade of yellow. If the stone feels dead, burnt, or wounded, it is not suitable for healing work.

An interesting use of irradiated gemstones is turning quartz crystal into aqua aura crystal by irradiating it with gold. Opal aura crystal is irradiated with zircon, and rainbow aura irradiated with titanium. These stones are beautiful, and the healing properties seem to be enhanced rather than diminished by the treatment process. Again, it is up to the individual as to whether to use them for healing work or healing jewelry and on what occasions.

CHOOSING GEMSTONES FOR HEALING

We choose gemstones for healing by how they feel. If the stone feels wonderful, it doesn't matter what its correct name is or where it comes from. A material that feels dead, uncomfortable, or inert is not good for healing, no matter what it is, and you won't choose it. You may pick a stone, decide that you like how it feels and then ask, "What is it?" People often ask me, "What's the right gemstone for me?" I always tell them, "It's the one you are drawn to, the one that feels so good you don't want to put it down." How a stone feels, or how it makes you feel while holding it, is the first criteria for what stone is best for you to use for healing. It is important to note that what feels good to you may not feel good to someone else. We all have different energies and needs.

How are gemstones used for healing? They can be used formally or informally. It can be as simple as selecting a stone that feels wonderful and carrying it around in your pocket. It can be as simple as choosing a pendant, earrings, or a string of beads that you are drawn to and wearing them often. Anything that brings the stone into your aura is the beginning of gemstone healing. A stone across a room from you is mostly outside your aura and not likely to be useful unless it is a large specimen that could effect the energy of the entire room. Larger stones are often good healing tools in a room where you spend a lot of time. Put the stone close to where you usually spend time in the room. For example, to help with peaceful sleep, place a larger (four inches or more) chuck of amethyst under your bed or on your nightstand.

You can use gemstones as altar objects as wands (or at the end of a wand) to cast a Wiccan ritual circle, or as objects to hold in your hand while meditating or doing psychic work. Use a crystal sphere, a raw piece of clear quartz, or another translucent colored gemstone, natural or polished, for scrying. (Scrying is the art of seeing psychic pictures by using a crystal to focus the meditation.) Gemstones can also be placed in a glass with a few ounces of filtered water on a windowsill overnight; after removing the stone, the water can be consumed as a gemstone essence. Do not do this with malachite, chrysocolla, or cinnabar as they are poisonous to ingest. Also, do not do it with angelite, halite, or other very soft gemstones as they may melt in the water. If you want the essence to last longer than overnight, add a teaspoon of brandy or vinegar to preserve the energy. For more information on making and using gemstone essences see my book *Healing with Gemstones and Crystals* (Crossing Press, 1996).

Gemstones are also used for making pendulums. They are traditionally placed at both the weighted end and the holding end of a pendulum, whether you make your pendulums at home or buy them in a store. Although gemstones are superior for a pendulum's energy-conducting ability, they are fragile.

They break easily and can become "dead" after dropping them or after a long period of hard use. Gemstone pendulums, and any pendulums, have to be kept energetically cleared to work effectively, as do all gemstones used for healing. (See my book *Pendulums and the Light,* Crossing Press, 2004.) More information on clearing gemstones and crystals follows.

Another use of gemstones is in laying on of stones for healing. In this case, the person receiving the healing lies flat on her back on a floor or massage table, and the healer places gemstones and crystals on her body. The color of the stones usually matches the color correspondences of the chakras they are placed on. For example, orange or brown gemstones (such as carnelian, brown jasper, or red aventurine) are placed over the belly chakra since orange (and alternately brown) is the color for that chakra. The stones are placed along the center line of the front of the receiver's body. Stones are also placed in the receiver's hands, between her feet, and above her head. The stones shift and fall off when they have done their work, which is to balance the body's chakras and entire energy system. More information on chakra colors follows.

DEDICATING AND CLEARING GEMSTONES

All gemstones and crystals, no matter what uses they are put to, must be dedicated to the Light and kept energetically cleared. This is essential. Quartz crystals and most colored gemstones absorb energy, and they will carry that energy until it is released. If you carry a stone in your pocket, it will absorb from you your discomfort, illness, emotional distress, tiredness, and other negative energies, while giving back to you the support you need. However, if you do not clear the stone, it will become overloaded with what it absorbed. It will then give back to you all the negatives it took from you, or it may shatter or even disappear from your pocket or room. Beads break, a stone that was on your dresser when you went to bed is gone in the morning, the pendulum won't work well or at all, and the crystal or colored gemstone cracks, disintegrates, or chips.

Clearing is a simple thing to do. The most common crystal clearing technique is to place the crystal, beads, pendulum, or other stone in a bowl of dry sea salt overnight or soak it for an hour in a strong sea salt-and-water solution. Salt can be too harsh for jewelry, however, as it will eventually rot the cord the beads are strung on and turn silver black. Placing jewelry or pendulums under a pyramid works beautifully, but it can take as long as three days to clear them. Placing stones in sunlight or moonlight, under running water, on a clean patch of ground outdoors, or passing them through incense smoke are other clearing methods. Avoid direct sunlight for amethyst, citrine, kunzite, and rose quartz, as they will fade. Avoid water (with or without salt) for angelite or halite, as they melt. Stones should be cleared after every use, and if you wear or carry them in your aura all day they should be cleared every night.

When you bring home a new crystal or gemstone, it should be dedicated to the Light, even before its first clearing. This can be as simple as holding the stone in your hand and making the statement, "I dedicate this gemstone to the Light." If you know Reiki, do a Reiki attunement over the gemstone or crystal while making the statement. You can do a more formal ritual for this but it is unnecessary. Just stating the intent is enough. Declaring such intent allows Light Be-ings, such as angels and spirit guides, to work through the stone to help heal you. It also prevents anything not of the Light from using the stone or harming you through it. This simple act is necessary and important. I dedicate every stone, crystal, bead strand, piece of jewelry, or pendulum I bring into my home. If I make raw materials into pendulums or jewelry, I repeat the dedication for the finished item.

The gemstone uses that are described in this book have been derived by channeling. They do not depend on the traditional uses of stones or those determined in other books or by other people. Most of the stones listed are relatively new on the market and often do not have traditional references. This book is the result of a gemstone database that I have kept and added to for a number of years. The definitions are brief and concise and meant to be a guide rather than the last and only word on any entry. You might find other uses for some stones.

The information I provide comes directly from a Light-Be-ing who choses to give the information. Such information is fresh and new, not dependent on older opinions or anyone's authority. I usually held a stone in one hand, while writing down in a notebook what I heard about it. However, with over five hundred different kinds of stones in this book, I did not have specimens of every one of them to hold for the channeling. For some stones I relied on photographs from gemstone catalogs and the Internet, with the assurance that the information would still be accurate. When I have later held stones that I first channeled this way, their attributes came through very closely to what I determined they were when I used a photograph. A few of these stones are rare or very new, and I used them because they were beautiful or interesting to me; however, most entries are for readily available gemstones. New gemstones seem to be appearing almost daily.

UNDERSTANDING THE KUNDALINI AND HARA LINE CHAKRAS

Some brief information on the Kundalini and Hara Line chakras is in order here. The Kundalini chakras are the series of seven energy centers that run down the center front of the body, and most people involved with metaphysics and healing are familiar with them. These chakras are located on the etheric body level, the energy level closest to the physical body. Chakras are receptors that bring in energies from the Earth below and the Light above. How well we are able to process these energies determines our state of physical health. Each chakra works to regulate a different aspect of physical life, including our basic emotions and mental states.

Each chakra has a corresponding color (the alternate colors I often use are mostly for the Hara Line described below, except for the heart chakra where two colors are generally accepted). Since gemstones come in a rainbow of colors, their colors can be matched with the chakra colors and are used for healing the corresponding chakra. For example, if the heart chakra's color correspondences are green (traditionally) and pink (generally accepted), then green or pink stones are used when heart healing is needed. These gemstone energies support healing for the heart physically and/or emotionally. The definitions of which gemstones match each chakra, beyond the color correspondence, are not rigid.

Beginning with the **root chakra**, located at the genitals, the healing color is red. The root is the seat of the life force, survival and one's core identity, as well as the place of grounding, centering, and reducing one's anger. Red gemstones include garnet, ruby, spinel, bloodstone (red and green), and red jasper. Only a few gemstones occur naturally in this color.

Next is the **belly chakra**, located below the navel, whose corresponding color is orange. The belly is the seat of sexuality, birth, menstruation, sensuality, fertility, sexual relationships, desire (more than sexual desire), passion of all types, and some forms of creativity. Some corresponding gemstones include carnelian, poppy carnelian, vanadinite, peach aventurine, red-orange coral, Tampa Bay coral, mookite jasper, and orange agate.

The **solar plexus** follows, located at the waist between the lowest pair of ribs, associated with the color yellow. It is the place of perceptual feeling, assimilation of psychic impressions, digestion, physical energy distribution, and mental energy, intellect, and the mind. Stones for this center include citrine, amber (used more for the Hara Line), yellow jade, golden labradorite, sunstone, and tigereye.

The **heart chakra** is located beneath the breastbone at the center of the chest. Heart chakra healing involves the emotions, the physical heart, compassion for oneself and others, a positive self-image, and a sense of connectedness—understanding the oneness of all life. Green stones for the heart chakra include green aventurine, green jade, tree agate, dioptase, watermelon tourmaline, green fluorite and prehnite. (Aqua stones are for the Hara Line heart.) Pink heart healing gemstones include rhodonite, rose quartz, kunzite, peach moonstone, pink sapphire, pink Andean opal, pink Botswana agate, smithsonite, leopard skin agate (or jasper), and rhodochrosite.

The **throat chakra**, at the lower front of the throat, with its light blue color, brings healing to the physical throat, as well as healing and support for speech, singing, acting, writing, creativity, speaking one's truth, and speaking one's needs. Its primary attributes are expression, particularly expression of personal truth. Light blue stones for this chakra include blue topaz, amazonite, sodalite (also used for the third eye), blue moonstone, angelite, blue calcite, and turquoise (also good for the thymus chakra).

The brow, or **third eye chakra**, which is above and between the eyes, corresponds to a dark blue or indigo color. This chakra heals and supports vision, psychic vision, clairvoyance, perceptions of psychic and physical reality, whole body purification, and energy cleansing. Indigo gemstones stimulate psychic perception, but they may not work gently. Such stones include lapis lazuli, iolite, blue aventurine, blue fluorite, blue sapphire (also used for the Hara Line causal body chakra), and blue druzy chalcedony (also called avalonite).

The **crown chakra**, located just behind the top of the head, is the spirituality center of the physical-etheric body levels. It brings in energy and information from the Light above, and then provides all our impressions of what is beyond—our physical consciousness. Its color is violet or purple. Clear crystals and gemstones are often used for this center as there are very few violet gems, but colored gemstones include most varieties of amethyst, violet tourmaline, purple fluorite, and cabochon ruby (which is more purple than red and used to connect the root and crown chakras). Most people first opening to spirituality want to wear amethyst and keep it around them to the point of craving it.

The thirteen **Hara Line** chakras are on the emotional-astral energy body, a step further away from the physical, beyond the etheric body and Kundalini system. These chakras are less known but increasingly important in healing, since all healing these days involves emotional healing. More in depth discussion of the Hara Line can be found in my book *Essential Energy Balancing* (Crossing Press, 2000), along with information on other energy body levels and chakra systems. From the top down, the chakras and colors of the Hara Line follow.

The **transpersonal point** is located beyond the crown, being a higher level of it, above the physical body. This point connects us with our core soul and with all energy components beyond the physical for higher level spirituality. Its color is clear, and this is where the clear or white gemstones often used for the crown really work. Such stones include clear quartz crystal, white topaz, white apophyllite, phenacite, selenite, diamond, white opal, Oregon opal, mother-of-pearl and white or clear tourmaline. This is a powerful energy center to awaken, and the stones that open it often make one spacey and dizzy. This center is about connection with the Goddess and the universe.

The next chakras are a pair behind each eye called **vision chakras**, which enable one to do laser healing with the eyes.

The color for these centers is silver or grey. Stones include grey moonstone, mica, clear fluorite, danburite, grey phantom quartz, silver metal, dogtooth calcite, and opal aura crystal.

Below that, at the back of the head, where the skull meets the top of the neck, is the **causal body chakra**. This is the seat of receiving spiritual information and manifesting it into useful and understandable form. It includes channeling, clairaudience, automatic writing, and communication from spirit guides and Light Be-ings. The color for this chakra when activated is crimson or red-violet, with corresponding gemstones being pink tourmaline, morganite, pink sapphire (also used for the heart), or gel lithium silica. Before this chakra is opened, its color is silver blue, and kyanite, celestite, or natural star sapphire are good examples of corresponding gemstones.

Next is the **thymus chakra**, the high heart that is the heart center of the Hara Line. This center is located about two inches above the physical breast bone, and it hurts when you press it. Its uses are to protect the heart and immune systems, heal grief, and protect the physical heart; it is also a bridge between the heart and throat chakras. This chakra's color is turquoise, and its corresponding gemstones include turquoise, aqua apophyllite, aquamarine, chrysocolla, Andean blue opal, and Russian amazonite.

The **diaphragm chakra**, lime green in gemstone colors, is the Hara Line equivalent of the solar plexus. This is the center for emotional cleansing and detoxification of emotions, and it is not a comfortable center to work with. Gemstones include green kunzite (hiddenite), variscite, chrysoprase (the gentlest of the stones for this center), and light green serpentine.

The **Hara chakra** is located between the kundalini root and belly chakras, which are on the energy level below it. It is the seat of one's life purpose and the stability to achieve and manifest it. It is the body's central balance point, and its colors are golden, gold-brown, orange-brown, or even dark red. The primary gemstone for this center is amber, but other stones include golden beryl, many of the jaspers, brown kyanite, zincite, and gold pietersite.

The Hara Line **perineum chakra** is equivalent to the kundalini root, located between the genitals and the anal opening. It is the first chakra of the grounding system and is about bringing one's life purpose into physical form. Its maroon colors correspond to gemstones such as cabochon ruby (also used for the kundalini root and crown chakras), amethyst coated with red hematite (also a crown and root energy), red ruby, raspberry garnet, red obsidian, and spinel.

A pair of chakras called **movement chakras** is located at the backs of the knees. Their color is dark green or tan, and they aid forward movement on one's path. Stones for these chakras include moldavite, green amber, gaspaite, moss agate, salmonite, poppy jasper, several of the brown jaspers, and petrified wood. These chakras are also part of the grounding system, but the grounding chakras are located on the bottoms of both feet. Their color is brown, and they represent our connection to the physical world. All the brown jaspers operate here, as well as other brown and brown-and-black mixed gemstones, including lodestone, magnetite, and brown pietersite.

Below the feet, beyond the physical body, is the **Earth chakra** or Earth star which connects us to and with the planet itself. This chakra's color is black, and there are many black stones that help with this vital connecting—without which we are no longer alive. Gemstones include black tourmaline, tourmaline quartz, black onyx, jet, black jade, all the black obsidians (mahogany, purple sheen, rainbow, and snowflake), hematite, and pyrite with magnetite (sometimes called healer's gold or Apache gold).

Many gemstones have more than one chakra correspondence, or can be used for both Kundalini and Hara Lines. The above is only the barest overview of the chakra systems referred to in this book. A few references to other energy levels may be briefly mentioned in the listings that follow, but for more in-depth information on several other energy system levels see *Essential Energy Balancing,* which maps and describes them in greater detail. Each of us is a far more complex energy system than we have knowledge of. Illustrations for the Kundalini and Hara Line chakras are located on pages xxviii–xxxi for reference.

USING THIS BOOK

The entries in this book take the following form: the name of the gemstone appears on the far left on the first line of the entry; the chakra (Kundalini or Hara Line) that the stone most affects for healing (although it is not the only possible chakra for that gemstone) appears in the center; and the stone's color or colors appears on the far right. Following this is a succinct description of the stone's uses for healing. While the format is brief, its brevity is deceptive—there is a lot of information here. If you wish to read about the traditional uses of many basic gemstones, see my book *The Women's Book of Healing* (Crossing Press, 2004, original printing 1986).

The information that follows is open to your examination. Verify it through your own experience, your own channeling, your own use of gemstones and crystals. There is no one "right" way of healing, only many paths and many questions with many lifetimes of inquiry needed to respond to them.

ILLUSTRATION 1.

The Kundalini Chakras
Etheric/Physical Body

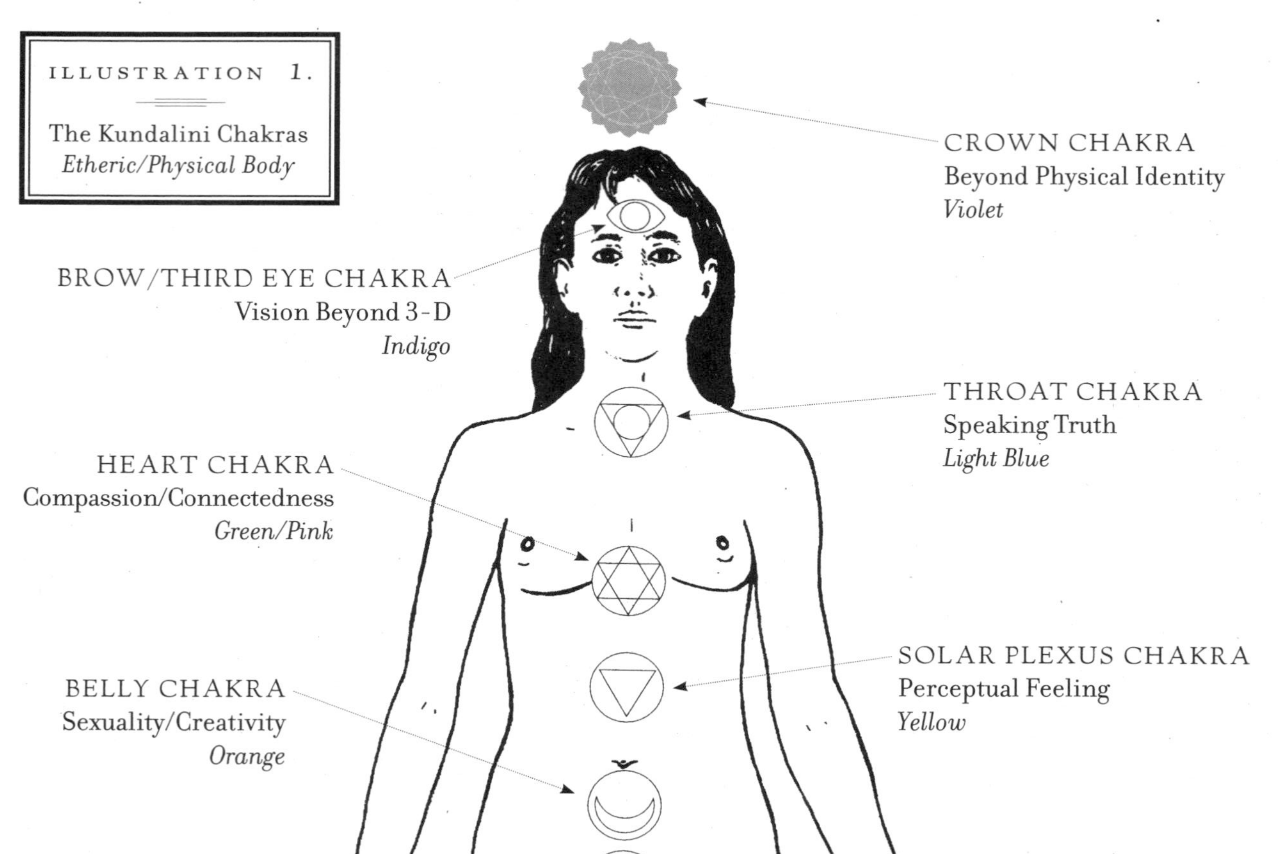

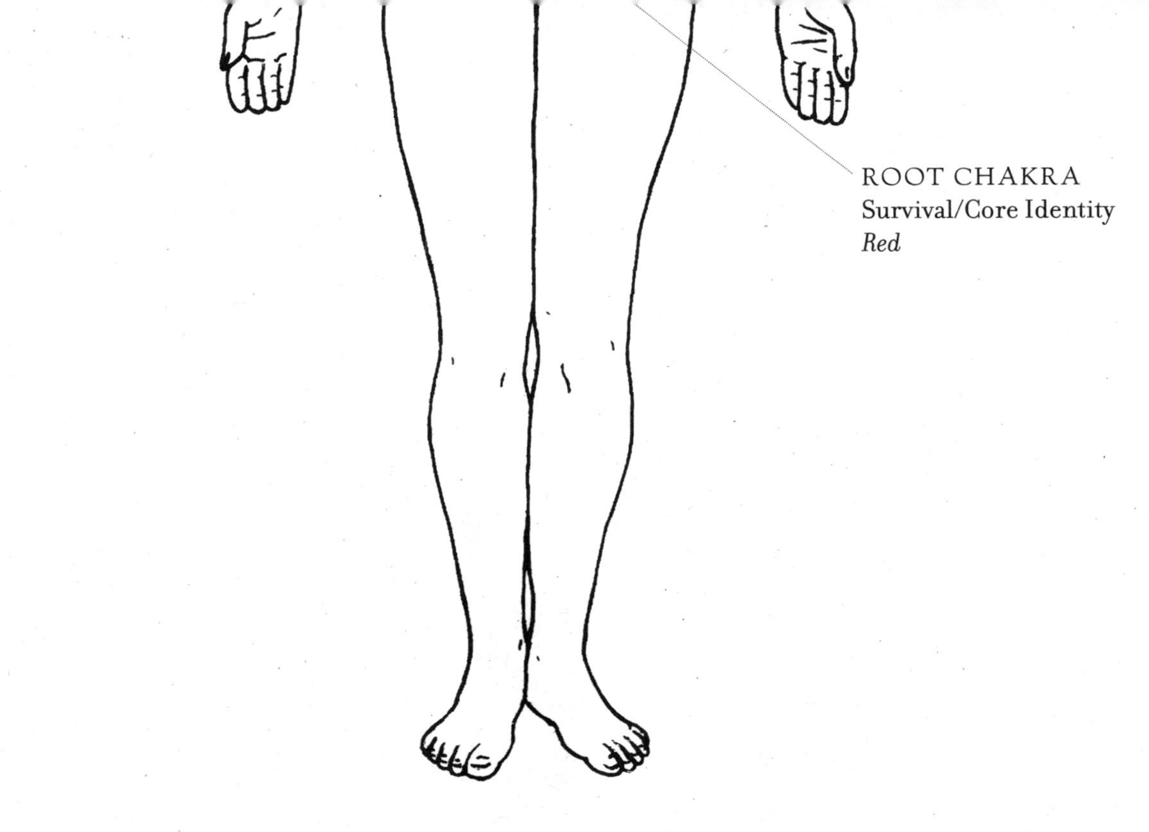
ROOT CHAKRA
Survival/Core Identity
Red

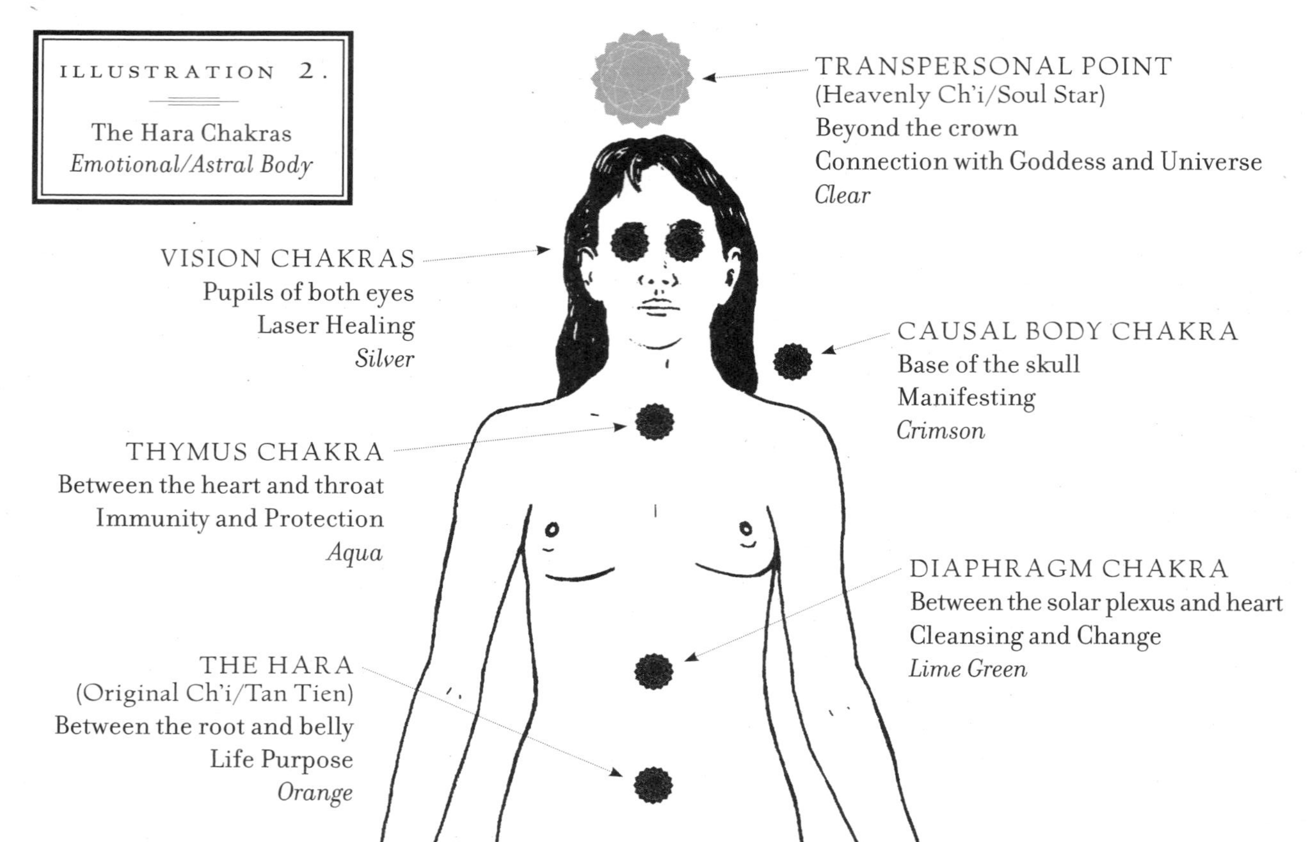
ILLUSTRATION 2.
The Hara Chakras
Emotional/Astral Body
TRANSPERSONAL POINT
(Heavenly Ch'i/Soul Star)
Beyond the crown
Connection with Goddess and Universe
Clear
VISION CHAKRAS
Pupils of both eyes
Laser Healing
Silver
CAUSAL BODY CHAKRA
Base of the skull
Manifesting
Crimson
THYMUS CHAKRA
Between the heart and throat
Immunity and Protection
Aqua
DIAPHRAGM CHAKRA
Between the solar plexus and heart
Cleansing and Change
Lime Green
THE HARA
(Original Ch'i/Tan Tien)
Between the root and belly
Life Purpose
Orange

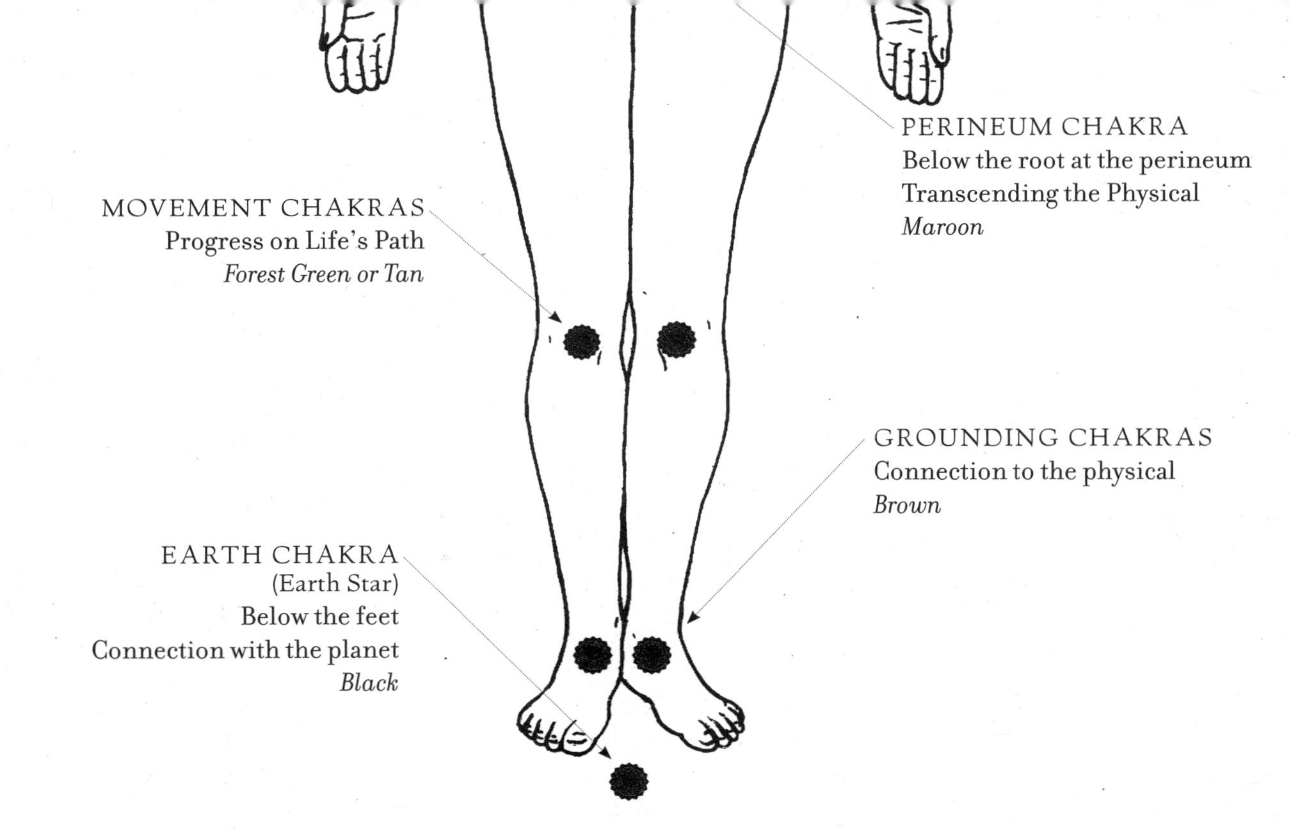
PERINEUM CHAKRA
Below the root at the perineum
Transcending the Physical
Maroon
MOVEMENT CHAKRAS
Progress on Life's Path
Forest Green or Tan
GROUNDING CHAKRAS
Connection to the physical
Brown
EARTH CHAKRA
(Earth Star)
Below the feet
Connection with the planet
Black

GLOSSARY OF TERMS

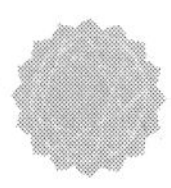

What follows is a series of brief definitions for terms frequently used throughout the book.

Akashic Record: The history of a person's many incarnations into physical body. When granted a karmic release by the Lords of Karma, you may sometimes see them erasing or writing the changes into your Akashic Record.

Ascension Body: The new body created when ascension is achieved. Ascension means that all karma and all evil interference have been cleared to a particular level (at least the Galactic level). The Ascension Body brings in one's Goddess (for women) or God (for men) if you have been chosen to join with a Light Be-ing. This is the goal of my *Essential Energy Balancing* book series, to achieve ascension and joining with a Goddess or God.

Astral Twin: An energy double of the physical body located on the emotional body level. She is who we really mean by our "inner child."

Bar Attachments: Drinkers are the target of discarnate entities that are addicted to alcohol. They were alcoholics when they were alive and they hang around bars as "ghosts." They can attach themselves to living people and cause or worsen alcoholism and create other havoc in people's lives.

Cross of St. Michael: Refers to karmic guilt and suffering that some people carry from other lifetimes, usually not knowing why.

Divine Director: A Light Be-ing similar to the Lords of Karma but who has the authority to release one's karma up to the Cosmic level. Once your Earth karma is cleared, Divine Director receives your karmic release requests for ending the karma of lifetimes on planets other than Earth.

Etheric Body Template: Doorway between the emotional and mental body levels.

Etheric Double: The Etheric Body is the energy copy of the physical body that is closest to our dense physical Be-ing. The Etheric aura can sometimes be seen as a thin red or black ribbon surrounding our physical body. The Etheric Double is similar to our "inner child" but is actually our "inner infant." The Etheric Double is usually merged into us, and we rarely have awareness of this level of our Be-ings.

Full Complement DNA: The optimal evolutionary amount of DNA strands to be connected for each individual on the ascension path. The amount depends on each person's soul evolution; as she evolves higher through the levels of karmic clearing, more strands are automatically connected.

Grids: These are an energy network that surrounds the Earth and to which each individual is connected. Imagine them like the longitude and latitude lines on a map, though there are fourteen grids for this planet and those who live here. Ley lines are physical extensions of these grids. Some of the grids are: the **mind** grid, **earth** grid, **interspace** grid, **Light** grid, and **protective** grid.

Hara Line scavenger and clean up: Atlantisite removes debris and old karma from the Hara Line, the emotional body level of our energy makeup. Compare it to a vacuum cleaner that removes "dirt" and brightens up the house. In this case, the "dirt" is old emotions.

Hooks and Cords: These represent karma with damaging people who have held on through multiple lifetimes. Removing the hooks and cords releases the attachments of these people, then the damage (the karma) from the people and their attachments has to be released and healed.

Ida, Pingala, and Sushumna: The three energy channels of the Kundalini Line. These are not the chakras but they move through the chakras; there is a central channel, a channel moving from root to crown, and a channel moving from crown to root. The doctor's Caduceus symbol depicts the channels and their movement.

Karma: Suffering from other lifetimes that has not been released or healed and therefore continues for no apparent reason in this lifetime.

Ka Template: Doorway between the physical and emotional body levels.

The Light: The goodness of the life force, the Source of Life, Goddess (or what you choose to call it).

Light Be-ings: Goddesses, Gods, Angels, the Lords of Karma, Divine Director and other high-level discarnate helping Be-ings who are the Light and serve the Light.

Light Body: The unified and merged Energy Selves (Higher Self, Essence Self, Goddess Self) that together comprise the Spirit. The Spirit (or Light Body) is the bridge that joins the body with the soul.

Lords of Karma: These are groups of Ascended Master judges who supervise one's soul evolution, and who have the authority to release and end karma and suffering.

Oversoul: Also called the Goddess Self, the highest expression of the Spirit below the level of the Goddess. An Oversoul contains, protects, and supervises an entire soul group or soul family of dozens of people who are and are not incarnated.

The Pleiades: We who incarnate in physical bodies—people—were created by the Goddesses when the Light was based in the Andromeda System of the Pleiades. Light Be-ings who still live in the Pleiades have a great interest in helping us and sometimes channel information and learning to us. Such information, if perceived accurately, can be extremely valuable for personal growth.

Silver Cord: The energy channel or trailing cord that follows one through life and is broken at the time of death. It is connected to the back of the heart.

Small lives: I use this term to refer to nonphysical Be-ings like fairies, brownies and devas. We usually don't see them, and they can be tiny in size when we do. Each has their job, however, and it is usually an important job for the sustaining of life on Earth.

Spiritual Noncommercial Manifesting: The term refers to manifesting that is not for money or goods but is for spiritual growth instead.

Templates: Doorways or gateways between the energy bodies.

Third Eye Counterpart Stone: This isn't itself a gemstone; it simply means that Azurite works for the third eye the way Dioptase works for the heart chakra to heal emotional trauma from past and present lives at the mental body level.

Twelve-Strand DNA: This is the amount of DNA that is connected when a person has cleared all of her Earth-only karma. When she goes higher than Earth in her karmic clearing, there are many more possible strands to achieve.

Void and Nonvoid: Buddhist terms to describe the raw material beginnings of creation. Everything, all possibility, comes from the Void (or chaos), to be made into form (through the Nonvoid) by the Goddesses, Gods, or the Light.

Violet Flame: This is a Light Ray energy for cleansing and purification that is in the keeping of Ascended Master St. Germaine. It is a powerful mediation tool for anyone to use.

Well of Life: The fountain of Water and Fire at the core of the Earth that is the center of the Earth's and each individual's life force.

Women's All-Healing: Refers to a gemstone that is an all-healer (does everything needed) for women. Some all-healers are for men and women, and a few are for men.

GEM STONES A TO Z

GEMSTONE LISTINGS

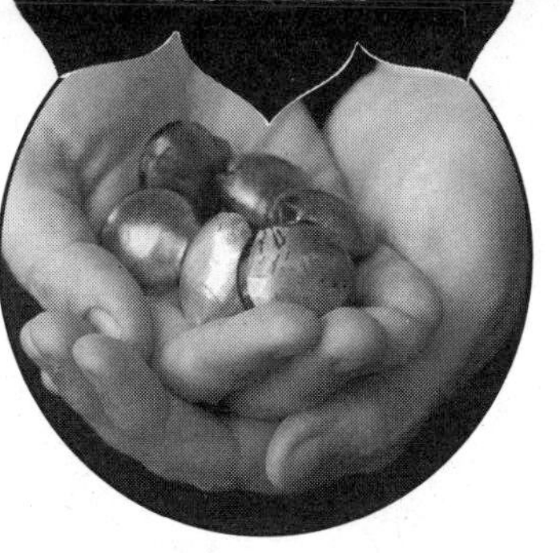

GEMSTONE LISTINGS

Achroite • *See* Tourmaline—Clear or Colorless

Actinolite • *(Movement)* • DARK GREEN

For taking action to manifest one's life purpose on the earth-plane; heals indecision, hesitation, fear of moving forward, and lack of confidence, lack of belief in oneself or one's abilities; stabilizes and grounds; offers certainty; aids in bringing one's spirituality into daily life in a calm and unobtrusive way; promotes quiet steady change and focus.

Aegerine • *(Earth Chakra)* • BLACK OR DARK GREEN

Also spelled Aegirine, alternate name Acmite. Used for protection from psychic attack, makes the wearer or place where stone is housed invisible to negative forces, repels evil; enhances self-esteem and self-worth, calming, centering, grounding.

A B C D E F G H I J K L M N O P Q R S T U V W X Y Z

Afghanite • (*Third Eye)* • BLUE

Promotes psychic vision and perception, visualization, and psychic opening; promotes the ability to perceive people and situations as they really are and enhances analytical, unemotional perception; aids psychic healers, but be aware that this energy is lacking in compassion.

Agate—Banded • (*Throat)* • LIGHT BLUE

Promotes creative analysis and problem solving, new and better ways to solve a problem or find a solution; promotes creative expression of all types, especially decorating and acting; enhances the ability to create sacred space and make any space sacred; aids in making one's life sacred; strengthens the courage to uphold and defend one's convictions, aids all service to the Light and humanity; resembles a labyrinth.

Agate—Black • (*Earth)* • BLACK AND BROWN

Connects Heavenly Ch'i to Earthly Ch'i, brings spiritual-level energy into the entire Hara Line and grounds it into earth-plane reality and consciousness; clears Hara Line of energy blockages; moves energy from head to feet, from spiritual levels and outer bodies into the physical body, brings spiritual awareness into action, balances Earth and sky, and stabilizes and grounds while elevating awareness; helps to clear emotional pain, for centering and focusing; aids nausea, indigestion, and cramps.

Agate—Blue Lace • *(Throat)* • BLUE AND WHITE

Encourages self-expression and speaking out, validating one's emotional truths; offers courage, aiding shyness and discouraging self-effacement; clears the throat chakra, programs the etheric body for creative work; heals laryngitis, sore throats, and hoarseness; opens the voice, soothes and calms.

Agate—Botswana (Brown) • *(Belly)* • BROWN AND WHITE

Good scrying and meditation stone, psychic balancer, grounds psychic abilities, and slows down clairvoyance and visions for easier comprehension; heals fear, grief, and hopelessness; aids insomnia by reducing worry; promotes understanding that everything will be okay and that *you* are okay in every way; provides comfort and security, knowing one is not alone.

Agate—Botswana (Pink) • (*Heart*) • PINK AND WHITE

Effects the heart like a stone thrown into a pool, sending rings and ripples radiating out to heal old pain; heals despair, heartache, and heart pain layer by layer; replaces pain with joy, heart healing and heart warming, calms, comforts, and provides security; eases stress; promotes unconditional love, knowing that one is loved; offers positive self-love and self-image.

Agate—Bull's Eye • (*Earth Chakra*) • BLACK AND WHITE

Grounds spirituality, moves energy from the spiritual bodies into the physical, manifests spiritually expanded awareness into focused earth-plane action, calms and concentrates a scattered life purpose and keeps it on target; aids real earth-plane achievement of worldly and incarnational goals.

Agate—Cathedral • (*Belly*) • ORANGE AND WHITE

Good stone for meditation and scrying, record keeper of the environments of the Earth, contains the herstory of the planet rather than of individuals; provides a record of planetary creation and birth; promotes visions of how the Earth and seas were formed; use it to meditate on the birthing of the planet.

Agate—Colorin • *(Root)* • RED

Aids women entering and progressing through menopause; provides support for women with uterine fibroids, heavy blood flows, weight gain, and hysterectomy; encourages acceptance of emotional and physical changes related to growing older; supports recognizing and taking one's power as a Crone.

Agate—Dendritic • *(Movement)* • GREEN AND CLEAR

Moves energy from the outer bodies and chakras into the physical level in a head-to-feet direction; aids in merging one's incarnational purpose with the planet's needs; focus on environmentalism, Earth awareness, and service to the planet; promotes activism and raising the mass consciousness; aids efforts to save plant and animal species, and heal nature.

Agate—Fairborn • *(Belly)* • RED-ORANGE

Supports all womb-related issues, including menstruation, menopause, menarche, fertility, pregnancy and childbirth, hysterectomy, and abortion; helps to heal all emotional issues centered in the womb; emotional hormone balancer; supports issues of femininity and being female; aids women's and girls' positive self-worth. *Note:* Relatively rare, this is the South Dakota state gemstone.

Agate—Fire • *(Hara Chakra)* • ORANGE AND WHITE
Brings energy from the spiritual outer bodies into the hara chakra; promotes spiritual awareness of one's incarnational purpose; strengthens the ability and will to manifest one's life purpose on the earth-plane; strengthens the will to achieve one's karmic agreements for this lifetime; aids stability and concentration, and manifestation of one's life work; increases energy and vitality.

Agate—Geode • *(Earth Chakra)* • BROWN, GREY, BLACK
Draws negativity, pain, and energy blocks through the chakra and aura layers to release them; suctions and vacuum-cleanses aura energy, acts as a magnet for negative energy and pulls it out; grounds negative energy into the Earth while cleansing and transforming it; has the ability to

self-clear (most geodes)—good tool for aura workers, massage therapists, and energy healers. *Note:* Geodes are also known as Thunder Eggs.

Agate—Green

Not found naturally, this stone is usually made from dyed Grey Agate.

Agate—Holly Blue • *(Causal Body Chakra)* • BLUE-VIOLET

Moves spiritual energy from higher levels into the physical level, opens and balances the causal body chakra for transmitting spiritual energy into consciousness, stabilizes spiritual energy moving into physical awareness; focuses one's life purpose and karmic learning plan for this incarnation into physical fulfillment; transmits higher-level information in a way that facilitates understanding; aids new channelers.

Agate—Leopard Skin • *(Heart)* • PINK AND TAN

Protects the heart chakra at the etheric double level only, brings spiritual energy into the heart to heal heartache and

A B C D E F G H I J K L M N O P Q R S T U V W X Y Z

heartbreak; protects healers from burnout and from getting overly involved emotionally with those they heal; promotes unconditional love; clears psychic attacks at the heart chakra level; slowly dissolves negative cords in the heart chakra, heals heart scars slowly.

Agate—Luna • *(Crown)* • PURPLE AND WHITE
Supports opening to spirituality, especially for those just beginning who are new and tentative on the path; aids gentle opening of psychic abilities; provides a gentle introduction and adaptation to a new way of living and thinking; works slowly, methodically, gently, and deeply; supports forward movement without being overwhelmed, progressing at a comfortable pace; aids moon meditation and women's moon cycles, living by the phases of the moon.

Agate—Moss or Montana • *(Movement)* • BROWN AND CLEAR
Brings energy from the outer bodies and chakras into the physical level by moving it from head to feet; makes spiritual knowledge and one's life purpose conscious; aids in incorporating one's life purpose and spirituality into everyday

action; promotes walking one's talk and living one's incarnational agreements, walking softly on the Earth Mother; helps nausea and ungroundedness.

Agate—Pitayo Cactus • *(Heart)* • PINK

Promotes unconditional love, self-love, and respect for all races and be-ings (human and nonhuman); aids seeing the Goddess in all Be-ings and seeing oneself as Goddess; encourages compassion and oneness with all of life, putting oneself in another's shoes, understanding how we are all more the same than we are different.

Agate—Plume • *(Vision)* • RED-BROWN AND WHITE

Good for meditation and scrying, for contemplation of life on others planets and under the sea; record keeper of the herstory of environments rather than individuals; opens psychic vision, visions of the past, and galactic herstory; offers a record of Earth's creation and the creation of the planets of the Milky Way; promotes a feeling of "going home" in the visions it provides.

Agate—Red-Brown • *(Belly)* • BROWN AND ORANGE

Calms belly chakra activity; eases sexual cravings; eases longings for a child and pregnancy; helps premenstrual syndrome, menstrual cramps, and nausea; brings on menstrual flow; calms emotions; slows, warms, and stabilizes.

Agate—Red Lace • *(Root)* • RED

Balances the root, belly, and solar plexus chakras; connects and heals the lower chakras, stabilizes the incarnation; reduces negative emotions; calms and clears fear, anger, and agitation; reduces greed, jealousy, envy, vengefulness and rage; promotes stopping to think before acting wrongly.

Agate—Sand Cast • *(Vision)* • WHITE OR BROWN

Promotes viewing oneself as an ancient Be-ing and one's life as a moment of the greater whole; provides awareness of many lifetimes and of life beyond the body as a soul; offers information on the between-life state; aids understanding soul structure and knowledge of one's part in the universal plan; awareness of spirit guides, soul families, soul mates, and Goddess.

Agate—Sunset • *(Crown)* • LAVENDER
Protects the link between the crown and the outer chakras; aids meditation, psychic development, and calming; aids dream work and dream recall; reduces insomnia; helps perfectionists to know when a project is finished and that everything is done well; promotes a feeling that everything is okay in one's world and one's deeds, a sense of balanced achievement; reduces nervousness and stress; aids self-confidence; provides support for workaholics.

Agate—Thompsonite Eye • *(Heart)* • PINK
Protects from the evil eye, psychic attacks, nightmares and other negative energies and entities; reflects negative energies back on the sender; aids the ability to see into other people's motives and hearts; provides good energy for people who are too nurturing or overly involved and need balance—it can resemble a breast rather than an eye; protects "bleeding hearts."

Agate—Tree • *(Heart)* • WHITE AND GREY-GREEN
Supports stewardship with the plant and nature realms; aids those who live and work cooperatively with nature; promotes

communication with plant devas and tree dryads, nature spirits, Earth spirits and animal spirits; good stone for gardeners, farmers, foresters, planetary healers and Earth activists.

Ajoite • *(Thymus)* • AQUA AND WHITE
Connects with the Goddess and the divine feminine; connects and communicates with individual Goddesses; brings in the Goddess; promotes awareness of oneself as a part of Goddess; raises self-image, self-respect, and self-worth, and therefore raises physical and emotional immunity; supports healing women's dis-eases and emotional issues, rape and incest recovery, grief, anger, and loss.

Alum • *(Crown)* • PURPLE
Promotes karmic cleansing; dissolves karma; facilitates spiritual and karmic release; aids clearing and cleansing from psychic attacks; cleanses the aura's magnetic fields; provides psychic protection; supports blood cleansing, physical and spiritual detoxification, purification, and energizing. *Note:* This material is extremely soft and fragile, and it melts in water.

Amazonite—Aqua • *(Throat)* • PALE AQUA
Soothes and balances the throat chakra and throat complex; aids self-understanding of one's inner truth and the ability to express it; aids speaking, acting, singing, writing, drawing, and painting; promotes all forms of creativity; removes writers' and artists' block; helps artists know what they wish to work on and how to go about manifesting their ideas and concepts; promotes inner peace, expression, peaceful confrontation, and saying what one means in difficult situations; reduces worry and aids the ability to flow with a project or situation; element of water, promotes psychic help from water spirits.

Amazonite—Russian • *(Thymus)* • DEEP AQUA AND WHITE
Aids the ability to release emotional body grief by expressing it as creativity; opens the connection between the thymus (emotional body) and throat (etheric body); promotes expressing one's deepest emotions to release, heal, and resolve them; aids concentration, helps in completing projects; supports writers, musicians, dancers, nonverbal artists, all artists; supports physical calcium balance via the parathyroid and thyroid; traditionally said to aid alcoholism at the nutritional level.

Amber—Black • *(Hara Chakra)* • DARK BROWN

Calms and clears the hara chakra and the entire Hara Line; protects from negative energy by absorbing and dispelling it; offers a sense of safety, security and peace; protects the Hara Line and emotional body; helps remove negative cords and hooks from Hara and Kundalini Line chakras, heals the damage from hooks and cords and prevents more from attaching; protects from psychic attacks and psychic vampires.

Amber—Cherry • *(Root)* • RED

Connects the Hara and Kundalini Lines at the root and perineum chakras; promotes life force assimilation, grounding, fertility, sexual opening, sexual desire, and orgasm; aids compassion and heals burnout; warms and heats; supports blood cleansing and uterine cleansing; cleanses the Hara and Kundalini Line channels. *Note:* Cherry Amber was a popular jewelry stone in the 1930s and 40s but is now becoming increasingly rare. Look for it in antique shops as antique jewelry.

Amber—Copal • *(Hara Chakra)* • BROWN-GOLD

Calms and protects the hara chakra and Hara Line; promotes a sense of peaceful acceptance and self-acceptance, "let go and let Goddess"; aids in gaining inner peace; soothes and comforts; provides emotional healing and protection; use it with Turquoise for protection and healing. *Note:* Copal is reconstituted Amber that is less powerful than Amber found naturally but it has its own energetic properties.

Amber—Golden • *(Hara Chakra)* • BROWN-GOLD

Stabilizes the entire hara system and emotional body; promotes certainty of one's path and choices; provides mental and emotional strength; balances and cleanses energy; provides all-aura healing; refills, protects, and repairs aura tears from too rapid emotional or karmic release, psychic attack removal, anesthetics, or other negative agents; shields against taking on others' pain in healing work; protects against psychic attack, psychic draining, or energy intrusion by others; highly calming.

Amber—Green • *(Movement)* • LIME GREEN

Clears the entire grounding system and its chakras and channels; promotes moving forward on one's life path, manifesting one's life purpose; removes blocks to achieving one's life goals; removes blocks to safe grounding; connection with the core of the Earth, connection with the Well of Life for spiritual nourishment; cleanses and purifies the entire Hara Line; repairs and reconnects the grounding system chakras

Amber—Honey • *(Hara Chakra)* • YELLOW

Calms and stabilizes; promotes quiet certainty of one's place in the world; promotes finding and accepting one's life purpose and path and the means to attain it; aids in knowing the truth, in separating fact from fiction or half-truth, knowing when someone is truthful; balances energy overload and overwhelm, prevents and reduces burnout; promotes the ability to "let go and let Goddess"; promotes having an overview of one's life in the past and to come.

Amblygonite • *(Solar Plexus)* • YELLOW

Stimulates mental activity; aids the mind, memory, studying, retaining information, and understanding concepts; promotes mind and mental healing; quiets mind chatter; aids the ability to focus; promotes alertness; calms the mind; increases functional intelligence; promotes analytical ability; reduces worry.

Amethyst—Brazilian or Mexican • *(Crown)* • PURPLE

Opens conscious access to the spiritual body, spiritual awareness and awakening; teaches that Be-ing does not stop with the body; aids conscious awareness of the soul, Goddess, and infinity; generates awareness of other-than-physical levels and realms, meeting one's spirit guides and angels; provides awareness of self as part of a universal plan, part of Goddess; promotes responsibility, self-worth, spiritual peace, and meditation; ease insomnia, headaches, and dis-eases of the head and brain; supports alcohol recovery; eases stress.

Amethyst—Canadian • *(Crown)* • PURPLE AND RED

Stabilizes the connection of soul and body, of spiritual with physical levels; promotes spiritual awareness manifested in daily life, spirituality as a way of living and Be-ing; grounds spirituality in the body; promotes understanding the wheel of life, death, and rebirth; understanding oneself as a part of the universe and universal whole, appreciating the oneness of all life; supports alcohol and drug recovery; eases headaches and migraines; provides stress relief; offers inner peace.

Amethyst—Canadian with Hematite • *(Crown)* • PURPLE AND RED
Stabilizes the soul-body connection; promotes spiritual connection and awakening, awareness of oneself as a spiritual Be-ing, spiritualizes one's earth-plane life; promotes seeing oneself as a part of the universal plan; aids karmic healing; helps to fulfill one's karmic agreements; provides contact with the Lords of Karma; offers karmic reprogramming and release; supports alcohol recovery and healing of other addictions, grounding, stress reduction, and endocrine balancing.

Amethyst—Chevron • *(Crown)* • PURPLE
Awakens one's spirituality; awakens psychic abilities; promotes a new awareness of yourself as a spiritual Be-ing, awareness of oneness with Goddess; guides those new to

spirituality, acts as a guide to teach them; purifies. *Note:* Amethyst is the primary stone to use for spiritual opening. Chevron Amethyst differs from other Amethyst because it works more on the physical level.

Amethyst—Elestial • *(Crown)* • LIGHT VIOLET

Opens all chakras beyond the crown and Kundalini Line, opens the intergalactic chakras; connects with Pleiadian higher Be-ings, calms and stabilizes; brings in other-planetary help, healing and Light; protects from negative alien energies and entities; energy clearing; promotes knowing that everything will be okay.

Amethyst—Green • *(Heart)* • GREEN

Also called Prasiolite, Green Amethyst is dyed Quartz Crystal. *See* Citrine—Natural for its properties.

Amethyst—Pink • *(Heart)* • PINK

Opens the heart chakra for giving and receiving; promotes positive self-image, body image, self-esteem, self-love, and empowerment; connects the heart and crown chakras for spiritualizing of one's life, one's emotions, and one's responses to others; promotes unconditional love and compassion; heals old and new traumas from this lifetime and past lives; heals the emotional body and one's inner child.

Amethyst—Rutile • *(Crown)* • METALLIC PURPLE
Aligns and raises the energy of the kundalini channels; clears energy flow and blockages in the Ida, Pingalla and Sushumna; balances and clears Ch'i flow to brain, central and autonomic nervous systems, lymphatic channels, and acupuncture meridians; aids awareness of this lifetime as one in a chain of many lifetimes, awareness of this life's learning and agreements as they fit into the soul's full incarnational plan; helps to heal personal karma.

Amethyst—Scepter • *(Crown)* • PURPLE
Purifies, repairs, aligns, opens the crown chakra to receive the Light; aids psychic opening and all psychic work; aids psychic transmission and psychic healing; promotes opening to spirituality, contact with Light Be-ings and angels, psychic development, and evolution; supports the head and brain;

eases migraines, headaches, and mind and mental disorders; promotes relaxation and stress reduction.

Amethyst—Smoky • *(Earth)* • PURPLE AND GREY

Brings spiritual certainty into physical levels and conscious awareness; protects from psychic attacks, negative entities, and negative alien energies; acts as a gatekeeper to prevent the entrance of negative energy while drawing in positive energy and help; contacts spirit guides and angels; aids in readiness for channeling; grounds after channeling and psychic work; promotes conscious spiritual growth; aids meditation.

Ametrine • *(Crown)* • PURPLE AND GOLD

Stabilizes the balance between spirituality and daily life; aids in bringing spiritual values and abilities into daily use; promotes spirituality as a way of life; promotes psychic opening and development, astral projection, working with spirit guides, and meditation; balances inward and outward energy flows.

Ammonite • *See* Fossil—Ammonite.

Andalusite • *(Grounding)* • BROWN AND BLACK

Connects and balances one's aura with Earth energy, offers balance in one's life, grounds, stabilizes, maintains balance and centeredness during times of adversity, reduces the tendency to create conflict with others or with one's true path, promotes keeping to one's spiritual path without argument or resistance, creates sacred space, invokes Pan and other nature spirits, protects self and home.

Andean Opal—Blue • *(Thymus)* • AQUA

Aids earth awareness and healing; encourages compassion for the planet and all that lives; promotes helping oneself, the Earth and all species through the Earth's changes; aids Earth healers and their work, helps individuals who manifest Earth change energy and trauma in their bodies and emotions; provides emotional body healing; supports inner growth and transitions; heals grief and loss, promotes achieving inner peace. *Note:* A tumbled piece of this stone resembles the Earth as viewed from space.

Andean Opal—Green • *(Solar Plexus)* • LIGHT GREEN
Connects the lower chakras (root, belly, and solar plexus) with the upper chakras (heart, throat, third eye, crown chakra); connects the energies of above and below; brings in the Light and grounds it into the physical body; connects the mind, emotions and body, helps make thought manifest; aids prosperity and abundance; spiritualizes one's thinking; promotes "walking one's talk."

Andean Opal—Pink • *(Heart)* • PINK
Promotes unconditional love, encourages compassion for all that lives, aids healers who manifest or feel others' pain in their bodies and emotions, heals Earth-change trauma held in the emotional or physical body, aids emotional body healing and heart healing, heals grief and loss, promotes inner peace.

Angelite • *(Throat)* • LIGHT BLUE
Stabilizes the emotions and the physical and emotional bodies, calms, enhances creativity and psychic ability, aids the ability to speak out for oneself and to teach or perform;

promotes connection with spirit guides and angels, aids the ability to hear spirit guides and angels, draws angelic protection to oneself and one's home, aids rebirthing, dispels anger, aids forgiveness and self-forgiveness, promotes psychic communication with people and pets, promotes channeling. *Note:* Angelite is very soft and will dissolve with prolonged soaking in water. It is also called Anhydrite.

Anhydrite—Blue

Also known as Angel Wing Anhydrite. *See* Angelite.

Anhydrite—Blue Druzy • *(Throat)* • LIGHT BLUE

Aids telepathy and empathy, animal communication, and communication with devas and air spirits; promotes contact and communication with spirit guides and angels, element of air; aids meditation, guided meditation, meditative journeys, and psychic healing; promotes empathy and compassion for all life; calms and comforts, aids oneness and knowing that no one is really alone. *Note:* Avoid soaking this stone in water, as it will deteriorate and dissolve.

Anhydrite—Purple • *(Causal Body Chakra)* • RED-VIOLET
Stimulates communication with those not on the physical plane—spirit guides, devas, angels, and discarnate entities; promotes communication with the Light; develops, connects, and opens the causal body chakra at the base of the skull; receives psychic information and healing, channeling, and automatic writing, increases all psychic abilities. *Note:* This is a rare stone from Madagascar, also called Purple Angelite. Avoid soaking it in water, as the stone is soft and will deteriorate and dissolve.

Anyolite • *See* Ruby with Zoisite.

Apache Gold • *(Earth)* • BLACK AND METALLIC
Aligns the body's magnetism with the magnetism of the Earth; promotes sensitivity to the Earth's magnetism, energy, and resonance; fosters a connection with the planet, planetary stewardship, Earth healing, and Earth awareness; brings psychic information into conscious awareness; aids intuition and the ability to validate and act by intuition; detoxifies the Hara Line energy channels; prevents and

eases burnout. *Note:* This stone is comprised of Pyrite with Magnetite and is also known as Healer's Gold.

Apatite—Blue • *(Thymus)* • DEEP AQUA

Detoxifies suffering from the thymus chakra and emotional body, reminding it is "not my pain but the world's pain"; eases the stress of carrying the Earth's emotions in the physical body; releases the idea of deserving to suffer; releases grief for oneself and the state of the world; aids letting go of pain to accept peace and joy; promotes appreciation of the Earth's beauty; provides emotional support for the immune system.

Apatite—Yellow • *(Diaphragm)* • YELLOW GREEN

Detoxifies negative emotions relating to self-image—feeling ugly, shy, shame, guilt, or not good enough; releases karmic guilt and the "Cross of St. Michael"; releases karmic suffering; releases the feeling that one deserves pain, poverty, and misfortune; allows one to accept love, comfort, support, and self-love; supports people with protective obesity; aids the ability to assimilate; cleanses the lymphatic, glandular, and meridian systems.

Aphrodite • *(Heart)* • PINK

Promotes opening to receive love and support from a significant other; aids the ability to give emotionally to a lover; helps draw a mate to you; promotes finding your twin soul relationship, forming a relationship, maintaining fidelity in a relationship, and trust and cooperation with a mate; heals heart scars and the emotional body; heals the damaging effects of failed relationships from this lifetime

Apophyllite—Aqua • *(Thymus)* • LIGHT AQUA

Heals grief and clears it from the emotional body; promotes inner peace; enhances the ability to accept and release loss and emotional pain; aids self-forgiveness and forgiveness of others; develops awareness of self and others as spiritual Be-ings; promotes awareness that the body is only temporary and only a small part of the soul's life; opens conscious connection to one's astral twin, the Light Body and oversoul; aids acceptance; promotes allowing the return of joy, knowing "it's okay."

Apophyllite—Black • *(Earth)* • BLACK

Grounds, stabilizes, aids proper connection with the Well of

Life and the Earth's core; repairs the grounding cord and all the components of the grounding system, stabilizes one's desire to remain alive, brings joy into every aspect of living, calms, promotes confidence and trust in life and living. *Note:* Black Apophyllite is a rare stone.

Apophyllite—Clear • *(Transpersonal Point)* • CLEAR

Brings spiritual consciousness to physical-level awareness, unifies and aligns the aura bodies, creates awareness of oneself as a spiritual Be-ing of far greater magnitude than the earth-plane level only; brings one's astral twin into the physical-etheric body level; opens connections to one's Light Body and oversoul; heals soul fragmentation, aids soul retrieval, promotes development and connection of full-complement DNA, fills the aura and aura bodies with light, promotes joy.

Apophyllite—Golden with Celestite

(Entire Hara Line) • GOLD AND BLUE

Amplifies spiritual consciousness; opens and heals the Light Body and Higher Self; clears connections to the Higher Self, Essence Self, Goddess Self/Oversoul and Goddess; clears the energy bodies (physical, emotional, mental, and spiritual); clears and opens the silver cord, initiates core soul healing; heals and reconnects full-complement DNA; promotes knowing who you are as a spiritual Be-ing; aids a sense of joy and purpose in living.

Apophyllite—Green • *(Heart)* • GREEN

Opens the heart to joy and love; heals heartache and heartbreak, heals the jaded heart; renews one's joy in life; renews one's ability to love and receive love; aids the ability to receive all the good things in life—prosperity, friendship, love, relationships, abundance, marriage and children; aids total heart healing, promotes a joyful heart.

Apophyllite—Red • *(Root)* • RED

Activates the life force with great joy and excitement; brings joy, eagerness, and zest for living into one's life; aids people not sure they wish to remain on Earth; heals burnout and disappointment; promotes connection to the Well of Life and Fire of Life at the Earth's core; stabilizes the incarnation and will to live; supports those with low vital energy, such as chronic fatigue or leukemia.

Aqua Aura Crystal • *(Throat)* • IRIDESCENT BLUE

Brings Light into the throat chakra, heals the ability to feel and express emotions, increase awareness of inner truth, heals the inability to speak out and the fear of speaking out, heals karmic structural damage to the throat chakra, aids telepathy and empathy, opens awareness of one's spiritual life. *Note:* Aqua Aura Crystal is made by irradiating and bonding Clear Quartz Crystal with gold.

See also Opal Aura Crystal, Cobalt Aura Crystal, Rainbow Aura Crystal, Rose Aura Crystal and Silver Aura Crystal.

Aquamarine • *(Thymus)* • AQUA

Fills the Hara Line with healing Light that reaches the Kundalini Line via the thymus; connects hara and kundalini channels and chakras; provides intense physical, emotional and karmic release, and supports one through the process; aids a life path of service; shields and protects with ocean Goddess energy; reminder of the love and caring of the Goddess in times of change and on one's life path; aids communication with spirit guides and angels; promotes connection with the Oversoul;

encourages spiritual and psychic awareness; heals and repairs core soul; aids soul retrieval; heals deeply at all levels.

Aragonite • *(Vision)* • GREY AND LAVENDER
Promotes the return to reality after euphoric states, effects grounding into truth, bursts the bubble of falsehood, promotes seeing what is real—like it or not, overcomes illusions and delusions, aids facing the unvarnished truth, aids in accepting reality. *Note:* This is not a gentle energy; use it in moderation.

Aragonite—Banded • *(Hara Chakra)* • GOLDEN TAN
Opens conscious knowledge of this incarnation's life purpose, returns one to the path after having strayed; recalls one's mortality and immortality, reminds one of life's realities and one's duties in this lifetime, balances energy, calms and stabilizes, heals procrastination and wasted time and energy, dispels one's illusions—sometimes harshly.

Aragonite—Blue • *(Throat)* • LIGHT BLUE
Strips away illusions about one's self and one's life; reopens

old wounds in order to heal them; exposes what is wrong so it can be made right; encourages telling one's story to heal it—a good stone when in therapy, comforting but intense; fosters speaking out and telling all; opens throat blocks; heals past trauma and abuse; aids incest survivors and those who have been forced to keep negative secrets. *Note:* This stone's energies can be harsh; it is best used in moderation.

Astrophyllite • *(Movement)* • IRIDESCENT BLACK
Supports knowing when to stop or start a project or activity; removes obstructions from one's life path and from one's movement forward on one's path; aids staying on one's path; promotes timing, appropriateness, knowing what is or is not for one's best good; helps in avoiding distractions, procrastination, and being sidetracked.

Atlantisite • *(Diaphragm)* • GREEN AND PURPLE
Purges and purifies the Hara and Kundalini Lines, Hara Line scavenger and cleanup, removes debris from old damage and negativity, dissolves negativity and blockages, repairs the energy channels, neutralizes toxins; filters energy coming

through the Hara Line to the Kundalini levels, helps keep the Hara and Kundalini Lines free of negativity.

Aurichalcite • *(Thymus)* • AQUA
Cleanses the thymus chakra and the emotional body of old and outmoded emotions; rebalances and refills with calm, certainty, positivism, and Light; provides inner peace and peace with oneself and one's life; heals grief and regrets; heals longings for the lost past; soothes and stabilizes; builds the immune system.

Avalonite (Blue Druzy Chalcedony) • *(Third Eye)* • BLUE-VIOLET
Opens the mythical past, the ancient archetypes of the collective consciousness, legends and lore, folklore and fairy tales—tales of King Arthur and Guinevere, Morgan Le Fay, druids, wise women, fairies, elves, and Goddesses; opens ancient wisdom and teaching for present day use; provides awareness of the magick of the past and knowledge that magick is still with us, using magick now via psychic awareness and the awareness of being of a long line of psychic and magickal women; aids meditation and visualization, calms and soothes, gives a feeling of security.

Aventurine—Blue • *(Third Eye)* • DARK BLUE

Teaches, heals, and regenerates; moves the wounded inner child from the belly chakra and heals her into the heart, supporting inner child work and inner healing; heals the emotional and mental bodies; heals the emotions via the mind and the universal Goddess mind; heals the Goddess within; promotes development of the Light Body and the mental body grid; aids connection with spirit guides and high-level healers; releases space junk and artifacts from the aura, releases negative entities and attachments from the aura and chakras; aids karmic release and karmic healing; promotes working with the Lords of Karma.

Aventurine—Green • *(Heart)* • GREEN

Promotes the ability to open one's heart to others and to trust life, to be lighthearted, and to take emotional risks; cleanses the heart chakra of fear; soothes physical and emotional heart pain; promotes a sense of emotional safety and security; support for all heart dis-eases and infections; promotes adventures in love and travel.

Aventurine—Peach • *(Belly)* • PEACH

Encourages playful sexuality; supports creativity—conceiving a child or other creative effort, sustaining creativity or fertility from conception to birth, enabling a gentle and joyful pregnancy or creative process; helps to sustain new ideas, aids in manifesting new life or new art onto the earth-plane; recommended for mothers, photographers, visual artists, potters, and painters.

Aventurine—Red • *(Root)* • RED

Promotes a joyful love of life, seeing the joy in every aspect of one's life and being; encourages gratitude, unconditional love, a zest for living, and "good energy"; aids living in the moment, living life to the fullest; aids the ability to take emotional risks without being reckless; promotes finding the joy, Light and goodness in everyone and everything; promotes making lemonade when life brings lemons.

Azurite • *(Third Eye)* • DARK BLUE

Heals emotional trauma from present and past lives at the mental body level; promotes karmic healing of negative energy patterns brought from other lifetimes; initiates intense transformation and transcendence; encourages breakthroughs when a healing process seems stuck; causes an active and conscious connection to one's Light Body and the planetary mind grid, to the Void and Nonvoid; provides connection with spirit guides, angels, extra-planetary helpers, and the Goddess; dissolves blocks and negativity; heals confusion; aids Earth healers, meditators, and psychics; increases psychic healing ability and visualization. *Note:* This is the third eye counterpart of Dioptase, which heals the heart chakra.

Azurite-Malachite • *(Thymus)* • GREEN AND BLUE
Connects the Hara to the Kundalini Line at the thymus (Hara Line heart), serves as a cleanser and astringent for both the Hara and Kundalini systems; boosts immunity; promotes emotional breakthroughs; clears the body of emotion-caused dis-ease, promotes inner transformations; brings karmic patterns into conscious awareness for releasing and healing; promotes thymus chakra opening, cleansing, and releasing; helps to heal past-life traumas.

Barite—Green • *(Diaphragm)* • YELLOW-GREEN
Promotes the connection of mind and body; repairs, heals, and reconnects; makes one aware of the emotions and events that hold one back; aids honest self-analysis, removes illusions gently, shows the source of difficulties in one's life; shows up negative and illusory thinking and helps to clear it; promotes inner truth that leads to change and inner peace.

Barite—Peach • *(Hara Chakra)* • PEACH AND BLACK
Clears, expands and develops the hara chakra; clears blocks and hara hooks; clears obstacles to achieving one's life path; increases heat, Ch'i and energy; brings energy from Hara Line channels and grounds it safely into the hara chakra; calms scattered energy; conserves energy; recommended for those who are scattered or who have low vitality, chronic fatigue or exhaustion; aids gentle balanced energy flow.

Beryl—Golden • *(Diaphragm)* • YELLOW
Soothes after long-term healing and emotional-release work, calms and aligns the emotional body, aids in balancing sustained changes and energy expansions, heals one's astral body twin and

brings it into the physical aura, supports weary old souls and bodhisattvas through Earth changes, aids healers' burnout; supports women in the menopause process. *Note:* For other Beryls, *see also* Aquamarine, Emerald, Goshenite, and Morganite.

Biotite Lens • *(Vision)* • METALLIC GREY
Clears and balances the vision chakras; aids visualization, clairvoyance, seeing the truth in difficult situations, and separating truth from distortion; promotes clarity; balances too much psychic perception; reduces the overwhelm of too rapid psychic pictures or impressions, slows psychic images for easier comprehension; aids seeing what must be seen; promotes using the eyes as lasers for psychic healing; helps to clear cataracts.

Bismuth
Man-made—no attributes for healing.

Black Onyx • *See* Onyx—Black.

Blackstone • *(Root)* • BLACK

Heals grief of all kinds; promotes comfort, acceptance, and the idea that there is no ending and death or loss are only temporary separations; promotes the feeling that we are all one and no one is really alone; grounds without feeling weighed down or held back. *Note:* Blackstone is often confused with Black Onyx and Black Jade; both of these are shiny, while Blackstone has a matte finish.

Blister Pearl • *See* Mother-of-Pearl.

Bloodstone • *(Movement)* • GREEN AND RED

Forces one's focus onto the physical level and the earth-plane, shuts off or minimizes psychic perceptions and distractions, promotes courage in living one's life on Earth and movement forward on one's life path, prevents distractions from one's life path, aids earth-plane achievement; promotes psychic protection by shutting down the psychic centers, good for those frightened or overwhelmed by psychic impressions; traditionally listed as a blood cleanser. *Note:* Bloodstone is also Green and Red Jasper.

Boji Stone • *(Grounding)* • BROWN, METALLIC

Works from the emotional body level to clear and stabilize the entire aura system; heals negative feelings, negative emotional patterns and old pain; translates emotional changes into physical body healing; heals physical pain when used singly; opens the aura and releases blockages from the acupuncture meridians and human electrical system when used in pairs; promotes the free flow of Ch'i and balanced energy; eases structural-skeletal pain, arthritis, backaches, scoliosis, and osteoporosis; aids feeling supported and nurtured by the Earth.

Bornite • *See* Peacock Ore.

Bronzite • *(Grounding)* • BROWN

Aids the ability to make choices and decisions about one's life and life path, clears confusion by reducing choices to the essentials and to the one choice needed for now, promotes resolution to follow through with one's life choices and keep to one's path, promotes courage. This is a masculine energy stone.

Brookite • *(Perineum)* • RED-VIOLET

Opens the Hara Line perineum chakra for anchoring and grounding during out-of-body travel; makes astral travel safe, providing a safe return; stimulates safe multidimensional travel of all kinds; prevents one from entering unsafe situations or dimensions while in or out of the body and provides a safe exit; offers understanding of karmic lessons and karmic patterns; provides a reality check for one's beliefs; provides the courage to face reality and truth. *Note:* These are tiny red crystals that look like Garnet except for their symmetrical diamond shape and markings.

Calcite—Amber or Honey • *(Hara Chakra)* • DARK YELLOW

Intensifies the circuit of Ch'i through the Hara Line channels and chakras; stimulates the Ch'i kung microcosmic orbit; opens the Hara Line chakras for spiritual soul growth; brings Light, information, and Ch'i from the outer bodies into the physical and emotional levels; clears energy blockages; stabilizes one's soul potential and life purpose; helps to heal ulcers and arthritis.

Calcite—Blue • *(Throat)* • LIGHT BLUE

Soothes the throat, eases the ability to speak out, heals throat center blockages and throat dis-eases, clears old traumas from this life held in the throat, supports peaceful assertiveness, eases shyness, promotes the ability to articulate one's needs, soothes anger, creates a readiness for peaceful change in one's life, promotes inner peace and quiet within, supports beginning spiritual growth.

Calcite—Brushy Creek • *(Vision)* • METALLIC GREY

Aids in using the eyes as lasers in healing, opens and focuses the vision chakras, promotes focus in one's life, creates one-pointed awareness and concentration, fine-tunes psychic perception, aids the ability to scan energy and see auras, promotes the ability to do psychic surgery.

Calcite—Clear Lemon • *(Solar Plexus)* • YELLOW

Cleanses, purifies, and detoxifies; aids emotional and mental clarity; promotes heightened awareness; enhances one's perception of what's true; promotes certainty and sureness, memory enhancement and quick thinking; supports blood cleansing and blood sugar balancing; aids those with diabetes or hypoglycemia. *Note:* Unlike other Yellow, Golden or Orange Calcites, this one is clear and transparent.

Calcite—Dog Tooth • *(Vision)* • WHITE
Promotes perception and focus; a psychic surgery tool for opening the aura and clearing energy blocks; it opens and focuses the vision chakras—a tool for using the eyes as lasers in healing, fine tunes psychic perception and visualization ability, aids concentration, eases neurological imbalances and misalignments, supports physical and psychic vision.

Calcite—Green • *(Diaphragm)* • LIGHT GREEN
Brings a flow of light through the diaphragm chakra to "wash" and clear it; intensifies the cleansing of old pain and negative emotions from the emotional body, speeds clearing of negativity from the emotional body and Hara Line; detoxifies physical and emotional levels, detoxifies pollutants and toxins from the meridian system.

Calcite—Mangano • *(Heart)* • PINK AND WHITE

Promotes gentleness, unconditional love, positive self-image, and appropriate behavior; eases shyness, fearfulness, agitation, and wildness; promotes aware innocence, an open heart, playfulness, and cooperation with others. *Note:* Calcite is recommended for children, however, it is very soft and will not withstand rough handling by a child; it is also too soft for use in jewelry. Place it in a child's bedroom or under her bed.

Calcite—Optical • *(Transpersonal Point)* • CLEAR

Opens and clears the transpersonal point and crown chakra for a greater ability to see and accept higher levels of spiritual energy; fills the aura with Light, clears attachments and entities, opens the whole Hara Line and hara chakra system; promotes visions of spiritual rather than physical reality, fosters trust in the opening and trust in new ways of seeing.

Calcite—Orange • *(Belly)* • LIGHT ORANGE

Soothes and heals past-life pictures of old traumas held in the belly chakra; helps to heal and release sexual abuse from past lives, aids in releasing karmic negative behaviors and personality problems resulting from past life traumas and abuse, clears negative karmic patterns, heals current-life sexuality, supports the healing of past abuse and of being battered in this lifetime.

Calcite—Orange-Banded • *(Solar Plexus)* • YELLOW-ORANGE
Calms and soothes like butterscotch or honey, reduces worry and anxiety; reduces mind chatter and obsessive thinking; allows one to "let go and let Goddess", promotes a quiet mind, inner peace, and rest; promotes knowing that whatever is wrong will pass and that everything will be okay; eases indigestion, nausea, and insomnia.

Calcite—Pink • *(Heart)* • PINK
Rebuilds the heart chakra and emotional body after releasing old traumas; refills the heart with love, self-love, and Light after releasing past-life and current-life pain; heals and repairs the heart after clearing heart scars; teaches new trust; helps the healed inner child; aids the healed and regenerated heart; soothes and offers hope.

Calcite—Ram's Horn • *(Crown)* • WHITE

Supports the healing and strengthening of bones and the skeletal system, the spine, joints, tendons, ligaments, and connective tissue; balances the immune and lymphatic systems; promotes calcium metabolism; eases arthritis; promotes emotional calming and centering, inner stability, and peace.

Calcite—Red Phantom • *(Root)* • ORANGE AND RED

Sustains courage and the will to live, supports people with life-threatening dis-eases, promotes the courage to die and be reborn, supports the courage to see an incarnation through to its fulfillment and conclusion, provides the courage to stay in one's body and face one's life, aids grounding, strengthens the life force, promotes one's ability to survive.

Calcite—White Snow • *(Crown)* • WHITE

Purifies, connects, repairs, and opens the crown chakra; brings in Light energy; connects with Light Be-ings; filters what enters to a comfortable and safe level; prevents overload, soothes and comforts; aids trust; reduces fear of being psychic, reduces fear of psychic visions and experiences. Recommended for people who are newly opened psychically and need to learn and experience slowly and in increments.

Calsilica—Rainbow • *See* Rainbow Calsilica.

Carnelian • *(Belly)* • ORANGE

Provides emotional support for all women's reproductive issues; stimulates, balances, and heals women's reproductive systems—uterus, ovaries, fallopian tubes, cervix, and vagina; eases premenstrual syndrome, irregular menstrual cycles, cramps, brings on periods; helps girls at menarche to appreciate their bodies and women to value and respect their life-making ability; promotes responsible sexuality, sacred sex, and planned reproduction; aids creativity of all sorts; elevates moods; warms; eases noninflammatory arthritis.

Carnelian—Poppy • *(Belly)* • PEACH, PINK

Promotes the sacredness of home and family; supports the mother-child bond, new mothers, and pregnancy, eases fear of parenting; helps infants adjust to their new bodies; promotes acceptance of incarnation; aids children who wish to leave their families; eases children's resistance to discipline; provides emotional support for asthmatic children and adults.

Cavansite • *(Third Eye)* • BLUE

Stimulates and opens the third eye for all forms of psychic work; opens psychic vision, clairvoyance, visualization, and psychic analysis; aids intuition, psychic information access, and the ability to see psychically what's wrong in the energy systems; good stone for psychic healers; purifies and protects from negative energies especially while healing or channeling. *Note:* Like Azurite, this mineral is delicate and soft.

Celestite—Blue • *(Causal Body Chakra)* • LIGHT BLUE

Heals the aura, astral body, and Light body; promotes connection with and the ability to work with Goddesses, spirit guides, angels, nature devas, dolphin devas, and ascended Be-ings; aids channeling; accesses information and the Light; promotes core soul healing, psychic development, twelve-strand DNA, and spiritual and karmic growth; aligns the energetic bodies; promotes peace, having the element of water and the ability to flow with life.

Celestite—Brown • *(Hara Chakra)* • LIGHT BROWN
Activates the hara chakra and all Hara Line and Kundalini Line chakras and channels; heals the etheric, emotional, mental, and spiritual bodies; promotes core soul healing focused upon the emotional body and Light body; aligns the energy bodies; anchors the higher self; opens the ability to bring channeled information into use in one's life; promotes connection with spirit guides, angels, nature devas, and ascended Be-ings.

Cerussite • *(Transpersonal Point)* • GREY AND PINK
Clears the silver cord and all the templates; clears the energy bodies; aids in anchoring in the Higher Self; heals soul fragmentation; promotes core soul healing; repairs split souls; heals reception and access to one's Higher Self, Essence Self, Goddess Self and Goddess; promotes ascension and spiritual evolution.

A B C D E F G H I J K L M N O P Q R S T U V W X Y Z

Chalcanthite • *(Throat)* • BRIGHT BLUE
Brings Light into the throat chakra and the entire Kundalini Line; clears obstructions and blocks in the throat; aids physical and psychic communication, telepathy and empathy, and psychic speech with other people and with animals; promotes dolphin connection and communication, and communication with devas and fairies; aids creativity, public speaking, acting; reduces stage fright. *Note:* This stone is very fragile, do not put it in water or place in direct sunlight.

Chalcedony—Blue • *(Throat)* • BLUE
Promotes peaceful assertiveness, peaceful well-being, and meditation; aids using speech, sound, and words to bring peace to any situation or the world; brings peaceful resolution to disputes; aids in being peaceful and in "being peace"; helps political demonstrators, performers, and activists maintain their peacefulness in violent surroundings; heals physical and nonphysical throat issues; promotes speaking out, enhances speech and creativity.

Chalcedony—Blue Druzy • *See* Avalonite.

Chalcedony—Brown • *(Grounding)* • BROWN

Grounds one into Earth consciousness; promotes awareness of the oneness of all life and compassion for all that lives; promotes awareness and psychic connection with animals, plants, insects, birds, and all Earth creatures; creates awareness of the suffering of all; promotes respect for the sacredness of all life and individual lives, knowing all are the Goddess; promotes the harmony of all lives together on Earth.

Chalcedony—Pink • *(Heart)* • PINK

Promotes compassion, heart opening, and heart maturity; honors the oneness of all life and the sacredness of all that lives; fosters awareness of the suffering of others and of oneself; creates awareness of Goddess and Goddess within; aids knowing oneself as a part of the Goddess whole, a child of the Goddess; promotes peace and harmony within, self-blessing, and women's self-image—a very feminine energy.

Chalcedony—White • *(Third Eye)* • WHITE AND CLEAR

Creates awareness of the sacredness of all life; promotes knowing oneself to be part of a universal plan and wholeness; aids spiritual growth and maturity, respect for the sacredness in every path, respect for the Earth and all that lives on it, and respect for oneself and others as a child of Goddess; fosters harmony within oneself and with others; promotes world peace.

Chalcopyrite • *(Solar Plexus)* • METALLIC GOLD
Encourages prosperity and abundance without and within; draws necessities and comforts; fosters the feeling of having everything one needs and wants; promotes awareness of inner abundance and the knowledge that abundance comes *only* from within; supports financial and material security, inner peace in a material world, nonmaterialism, and gratitude.

Chalcotrichite • *(Perineum)* • METALLIC RED
Connects the perineum and root chakras in the Hara and Kundalini Lines, stimulates the life force moving through the body; stimulates energy movement upward through the Hara and Kundalini Lines; opens and brings in Earth energy and moves it from the root and perineum through the crown and transpersonal point chakras; opens the kundalini chakras; raises the kundalini; stimulates sexuality; clears energy blocks

in legs, knees, and feet; warms and heats. *Note:* Very intense, a little of this stone goes a long way.

Charoite • *(Crown)* • PURPLE

Brings spirituality onto the earth-plane level and raises Earth energy to the crown chakra; spiritualizes daily living, promotes raised awareness of realities greater than the material and physical body; heals the body by making one aware of karma and a higher plan, aids responsibility, puts one almost forcibly on one's life path, heals people who selfishly control others by making them more morally aware, raises one's ethical levels. Recommended for a moral and karmic "kick in the (spiritual) pants."

Chiastolite Andalusite • *(Vision)* • BROWN AND BLACK

Contacts other realms of Be-ing—fairies, elves, devas, dryads, water spirits, animal spirits, and nature spirits; protects from people who are negative; protects from the evil eye; promotes learning and communication with other-realm Be-ings of the Light; aids understanding of other life forms, obtaining their help and offering help to them—a good stone for gardeners, animal healers, and communicators, Earth healers. *See also* Staurolite (Fairy Cross).

Chinese Writing Rock • *(Earth)* • BLACK AND WHITE
Record keeper of civilizations where people lived before they came to Earth, not a record of Earth but of other planets; provides information on one's own Akashic Record herstory of incarnations on other planets; may occasionally open up disturbing scenes and stories—meditate holding the stone but be careful about wearing it; provides information for karmic healing and release. *Note:* What is now being called Golden Lace Agate (or Jasper) was formerly called Chinese Writing Rock.

Chlorastrolite • *(Diaphragm)* • GREEN
Reprograms and repatterns the planetary mind grid and mind, heals negative habits by replacing them with positive ones, reprograms traumatic memories and incidents to defuse their power and promote healing and release, aids analytical ability, supports problem solving, helps those doing math. *Note:* This is a chatoyant green gemstone with striations that resemble a brain.

Chrysanthemum Stone • *(Root and Crown)* • BLACK AND WHITE
As above so below; balances the Kundalini chakras, helps to manifest earth-plane wishes and desires, helps in finding and holding a job, provides spiritual help for daily earth-plane needs, grounds.

Chrysoberyl • *(Crown)* • TAN
Repairs damage and tearing in the crown and third eye chakras and their associated connections, raises one's overall vibration and Light energy level and helps to keep it raised, cleanses and purifies the crown and third-eye chakras; aids connection with the Light, promotes angelic realm connection and communication. *Note:* This stone is beige or off-white with darker inclusions.

Chrysoberyl—Cat's-Eye • *(Vision)* • GREY-GOLD
Fosters the ability to see as a cat sees—all the things people miss; promotes visions of other realms, dimensions, and planets; promotes psychic vision; aids contact with positive other-planetary healers and teachers; promotes dream work, dream clairvoyance, and out-of-body journeys; promotes affinity and oneness with cats; aids psychic communication with small and large cats.

Chrysocolla • *(Thymus)* • AQUA
Supports women's all-healing and internal physical healing; promotes connection with Goddess and awareness of oneself as a part of the Goddess; connects thymus and throat chakras for releasing grief, sadness and fear from the emotional body; aids the beginnings of joy, certainty, and peace; promotes letting go, surrendering pain, and releasing worry to universal love; supports emotional healing from incest, rape, mastectomy, or hysterectomy in this life; supports healing for the lungs, throat, and heart; eases premenstrual syndrome and cramps; reduces inflammation.

Chrysoprase—Green • *(Heart)* • GREEN
Soothes heartache and loneliness; promotes emotional balance; aids conflict resolution, inner peace, inner strength, and courage in facing real emotions; promotes opening and healing old traumas and grief; encourages trust in Goddess and learning to flow with life and change; reduces fear and replaces it with unconditional love.

Chrysoprase—Lemon • *(Diaphragm)* • LIGHT GREEN
Facilitates cleansing and change; connection of Above and Below; connects with the green things of the Earth; aids communication with the planet and its life forms—devas, dryads, plants, insects, birds, animals, and people; promotes the understanding of environments and ecosystems—who lives there and what they need; aids knowledge of where the Earth is hurting and how to help; promotes compassion for all life, psychic union with the planet, and unconditional love.

Cinnabar Quartz • *See* Quartz—Cinnabar.

Cinnabar Wood • *(Root)* • RED
Stimulates the life force and the will to live; increases interest in one's life and surroundings; increases one's drive to succeed and to reproduce; promotes awareness of one's biological time clock; increases awareness of time passing and one's life passing with it; promotes longevity, physical warming, mood raising, anti-suicide, and anti-senility; increases alertness; focuses on earth-plane living rather than spiritual awareness.

Citrine—Heat-Created • *(Solar Plexus)* • YELLOW

Assimilates and digests energy, food, and ideas; supports the urinary tract; stimulates mental efforts; stimulates energy; moves energy upward from the solar plexus to open blockages in the upper chakras; detoxifies the kundalini channels; raises psychic ability by magnifying it; promotes understanding of psychic information; aids controlled astral projection; fosters self-awareness; promotes alertness. *Note:* Heat-Created Citrine is Amethyst turned yellow by heating it; most Citrine is created in this way.

Citrine—Natural • *(Solar Plexus)* • GOLD

Cleanses and detoxifies the Kundalini Line and the emotional body; supports tissue regeneration; offers spinal balancing on the meridian and energy levels by balancing Ch'i movement through the central nervous system; clears, expands, and aligns the aura bodies; heals, opens, and aligns the etheric, emotional and mental levels; opens the Light Body; fills the aura with Light and clarity; stimulates intellect and mental activity; eases urinary, kidney, and digestive dis-eases; aids assimilation. *Note:* Natural Citrine is yellow Quartz Crystal.

Citrine—Rutilated • *(Solar Plexus)* • GOLD AND METALLIC

Steps solar plexus energy up to a higher level; increases energy and Light information assimilation, greatly detoxifies and cleanses kundalini chakras and channels; raises intellect, psychic ability, and an understanding of psychic information; keeps one in one's body while meditating and doing psychic work; promotes self-awareness, enlightenment, and channeled writing.

Cobalt Aura Crystal • *(Third Eye)* • BLUE

Opens the third-eye chakra, stimulates psychic abilities and psychic visions; cleanses, purifies, and repairs; connects the third eye to the crown and throat chakras, enhancing the ability to understand and explain what one sees; good for psychic healing, aids healers' ability to analyze dis-ease and transmit Light. *Note:* Cobalt Aura Crystal is similar to Aqua Aura Crystal, but is irradiated and bonded with titanium instead of gold.

See also Aqua Aura Crystal, Opal Aura Crystal, Rainbow Aura Crystal, Rose Aura Crystal, and Silver Aura Crystal.

Cobaltite • *(Heart)* • DARK PINK

Brings Light into the heart, fills heart scars with light to dissolve them, "Lightens" heart pain and old traumas, relieves heart burdens, heals sadness and hurts, relieves those who carry others' pain with their own, helps bodhisattvas who suffer for others and the planet.

Copper • *(Hara Chakra)* • METALLIC COPPER

Grounds incoming spiritual energy into the hara chakra for storage and distribution, promotes balanced use and assimilation of Ch'i; grounds uncomfortable sensations and spaciness from too much psychic energy, reduces clairsentience, removes others' symptoms from one's energy; opens and heals the Hara Line chakras and the hara chakra itself; cleanses the emotional body of old negative emotions, provides emotional protection in crowds; traditionally used as a healer for arthritis.

Coral—Bamboo • *(Transpersonal Point)* • NATURAL

Supports bone healing; eases bone diseases, arthritis, osteoporosis, broken bones, bone degeneration, and bone marrow ailments; helps to build the body's structures; promotes the building of emotional support structures; develops and builds on all levels; promotes the building of support systems and support relationships in one's life.

Coral—Black • *(Earth)* • BLACK

Represents the Wiccan Horned God, the male son-lover of the Goddess; promotes male fertility, union with the Goddess, conception, and fatherhood; aids being the protector of the mother and child, protector of the family, and protector of the Goddess Earth; for psychic nurturing masculinity, the ritual High Priest that bows to the Priestess Goddess, the male who respects women and life.

Coral—Blue • *(Throat)* • BLUE

Calms, stabilizes, and reduces fear and insecurity; heals one's relationship with one's inner child; promotes inner child work and healing; aids in understanding children, learning to be around children, and learning to play with children as an adult; aids in expressing one's child self; helps women who suffered incest as children.

Coral—Indonesian Flower • *(Diaphragm)* • TAN

Soothes after diaphragm cleansing and purges; calms and settles after emotional trauma, especially after accessing disturbing karmic memories; releases old pictures and flashbacks of traumas from this or past lives; protects against the return of old karma; heals after releasing; comforts and stabilizes; acts as a karmic shield. *Note:* This is fossilized Coral from the South China Sea.

Coral—Pink • *(Heart)* • PINK AND PEACH

Supports pregnancy and giving birth; supports new infants; eases morning sickness; eases fear of becoming a mother and fear of delivery; helps baby feel wanted and secure; helps a baby adjust to a new incarnation; eases colic and crying, infant distress, and mother's postpartum depression; aids nursing.

Coral—Red Pacific • *(Belly)* • RED-ORANGE

Promotes conception and pregnancy, heals the ovaries and fallopian tubes, stimulates ovulation, draws a baby's spirit to its karmically chosen mother's womb, eases childbirth, aids a new mother's adjustment and bonding to her baby, aid's a new baby's entrance into incarnation; may also be used to aid the adoption process; heals an adult's inner child, heals adults who were adopted as children, helps mother-daughter healing.

Coral—Sponge • *(Belly)* • RED-ORANGE

Calms and balances the lower Kundalini chakras—root, belly, and solar plexus; stabilizes the emotions; provides an energy boost that is gentle and peaceful; promotes menstruation, orgasm, sexuality, fertility, easy pregnancy, easy labor and birth, gentle menopause—a good woman's gem; supports all the stages of women's lives. *Note:* This stone is softer than red Pacific coral.

Coral—Tampa Bay (Agate Fossilized)

(Belly) • BROWN-ORANGE-TAN

Calms and balances overactive sexuality; grounds instances of too-fast rising of kundalini energy; reduces kundalini reactions, spaciness, dizziness, hallucinations, hearing voices, frightening visions, heat, or creeping sensations; calms and soothes; brings understanding of what is wrong and how to ground it; grounds and centers.

Coral—White • *(Crown)* • WHITE

Helps children adjust to being in new bodies; aids their awareness of spirit guides and "invisible playmates"; stabilizes children's psychic abilities and protects them from being shut down by adult criticism; aids the physical body's growth; promotes optimal physical, emotional, and psychic development; protects vulnerability and innocence in children and adults.

Covelite • *(Third Eye)* • INDIGO AND GOLD

Creates and seals the ascension body, intrinsic in the ascension process; clears the templates on all levels; clears and heals the Tube of Light (one's soul structure); aids the spiritual, galactic, and causal bodies and their chakras; opens the third eye, promotes spiritual vision and clarity; stabilizes during the ascension process; promotes core soul healing; heals connections with one's Goddess Self (Goddess Within) and Goddess.

Creedite • *(Belly)* • ORANGE

Connects the lower and the higher chakras at the belly level; brings one's emotions into the body for awareness and healing; eases menstruation difficulties, especially preceding menopause; supports fertility in older women who wish a late pregnancy; heals wistfulness that one's biological clock is ticking out; heals fear of menopause and growing older.

Crocoite • *(Belly)* • ORANGE-RED
Sexual healing, heals sexual difficulties or dysfunctions; aids in healing the inability to sustain a sexual relationship; supports healing for venereal dis-eases, sexual addictions and aberrations; heals the womb and emotions of too many abortions; helps women who have suffered incest, been raped, or been battered to accept a new and healthy sexual relationship and partner; aids the return of hormonal balance after a hysterectomy.

Cuprite • *(Root)* • RED
A bright red stone that reminds one of blood; use for anemia, menstruation difficulties, regularizing the menstrual cycle and flow, blood circulation, fertility; supports healing from abortion, childbirth, hysterectomy, or other surgeries; supports healing from blood loss; a very feminine energy for women's issues, promotes entrance into women's mysteries;

meditate on this stone to learn about women's power in all its aspects. Red is also the Goddess Kali—destroyer of evil and champion of women.

Danburite • *(Vision)* • SILVER-WHITE
Intensifies, purifies, and magnifies all other healing energies; transforms negative energy and blocks into positivity and Light; opens the galactic chakras; opens visual awareness of other realms, planets, and dimensions; increases psychic vision; connects with the mind grid and Light Body; promotes connection with angels, spirit guides, oversoul, and positive extra-terrestrial healers and teachers; aids the ability to perceive beyond earth-plane awareness; enhances creativity and mental awareness, manifesting through the Void and Nonvoid; promotes gentle psychic opening at one's own pace.

Danburite—Aqua Aura • *(Throat)* • BLUE
Amplifies and purifies energy at the throat chakra; promotes creativity using voice—singing, speaking, acting, artistic expression; eases stage fright and artist's block; calms and centers while amplifying the power of every expression; aids

speaking out and speaking one's truth; makes speaking hard truths easier. *Note:* Aqua Aura Danburite is Danburite crystal irradiated and bonded with gold.

Datolite—Clear • *(Transpersonal Point)* • CLEAR
Balances one's ability to live beyond time while still living in the earth plane's time strictures, eases discomfort from time's speeding up in Earth changes, helps one to better use time without being time's slave, aids clock-watchers, reduces urge to rush, reduces time stress, aids in the ability to pace oneself, increases inner time sense.

Datolite—Green • *(Diaphragm)* • LIGHT GREEN
Connects mind and body to heal the past; aids memory; releases and ends flashbacks of traumatic memories; repatterns the planetary mind grid to heal past traumas by creating a chosen good memory to replace a negative one; aids analytic ability, especially for solving one's own healing of the past; helps healers to aid others in healing past traumas; provides the means for healing this lifetime's past as well for healing past lives.

Diamond • *(Transpersonal Point)* • CLEAR

Fills the Hara Line and Kundalini Line chakras and channels with Light, promotes connection with spirit guides and Goddess; combines one's marriage with one's life purpose, anchors a spiritual union with earth-plane bodies, fulfills the marriage contract made with one's mate in the prelife state, holds the marriage template, promotes harmony and balance in relationship and marriage. *Note:* A diamond retains a marriage's karmic imprint even after the relationship or the wearer's life ends.

Dianite • *(Throat)* • SILVER-BLUE

Promotes communication with other beings and other realms—animals, the Earth, devas, and nature spirits; promotes communication with the Light—the angelic realm, Gods and Goddesses, the Lords of Karma, and Divine Director; promotes psychic communication between psychically attuned people; aids and amplifies psychic communication and reception of all kinds, empathy and telepathy; amplifies psychic healing. *Note:* Dianite is a rare new find from Siberia that resembles Blue Labradorite; it is quite expensive.

Diaspor • *(Transpersonal Point)* • SILVER-WHITE
Reunites star families, provides a remembrance of home, clears the silver cord, aligns the aura bodies, clears the templates, aids merging in of one's Higher Self, develops and heals the Light Body, fills the Spirit and all the bodies with Light and healing, heals at the spiritual and causal body levels, promotes core soul healing, repairs soul fragmentation; calms, balances, aids all-healing, promotes ascension.

Dinosaur Bone • *(Hara Chakra)* • GOLD-BROWN
Promotes understanding of our most ancient herstory and roots; aids learning who we are and where we came from; uncovers origins on other planets, ancient civilizations, and one's place in them; accesses herstory beyond Earth and beyond written record; accesses knowledge of past lives in very ancient times; promotes accessing and clearing past lives and karma from incarnations on other planets.

Diopside • *(Heart)* • GREEN
Opens the higher intuition and higher mental body level; aids in the ability to honor one's intuition and follow its directions;

promotes the ability to feel and honor one's real thoughts, emotions, and feelings; opens the heart and mind to others; promotes compassion for the suffering of others and oneself; opens the need to help others and the Earth; provides support for heart healing; improves blood circulation; lowers blood pressure, reduces stress; calms.

Dioptase • *(Heart)* • GREEN

Releases past-life and current-life major emotional traumas; heals one's inner child; opens and heals heart scars gently; calms; relieves physical and emotional pain; heals the physical body by healing the emotional heart; releases past abuse; promotes karmic understanding; protects and returns lost vulnerability; affords a happy, playful energy. *Note:* Dioptase can self-destruct during intense healing work; it is an expensive, soft, very beautiful stone.

Dioptase-Malachite • *(Diaphragm)* • GREEN AND BLACK

Detoxifies traumas and heart pain from past lives for present-life healing and release, heals negative karmic patterns about heart and relationship issues, opens and clears heart scars;

brings karmic pain and patterns into conscious awareness for clearing, promotes lessons from past lives that are to be completed in this life, aids karmic release and karmic healing.

Dolomite—Orange • *(Belly)* • ORANGE

Heals fear; promotes courage and stability; aids facing one's fear and overcoming fears; opens the sources of fears and phobias to heal, release, and end them; heals the traumas that originated phobias and fears; promotes self-confidence and trust, knowing "I can do it" in all things; encourages trust in the Goddess; protects.

Dolomite—Pink • *(Heart)* • PINK

Helps the physical body metabolize calcium, easing osteoporosis, broken bones, and tooth and jaw dis-ease; opens the heart to trust oneself and Goddess; promotes inner certainty, self-confidence, and positive self-love; calms; reduces insomnia, nightmares, irregular sleep patterns, and night fears.

Dumortierite—Blue • *(Throat)* • BLUE

Opens and balances the throat chakra; eases self-effacement, shyness, and stage fright; promotes the ability to speak out; aids in speaking up for what one knows is real and true; fosters feeling secure, inner peace, and certainty; clears the throat and calms the mind; aids meditation; supports psychic communication with spirit guides and angels, pets and other people.

Dumortierite—Purple • *(Causal Body Chakra)* • RED-VIOLET
Repairs damage, tears, and holes in the causal body chakra; repairs damage to the causal body itself and its connections and system; promotes communication and information from the Light, trance channeling, and instantaneous transmission; aids the ability to learn higher truths and be tutored by Light Be-ings; opens advanced psychic abilities and the means to use them.

Eilat Stone • *(Thymus)* • DARK AQUA
Clears and opens the thymus chakra and balances it with the heart; detoxifies and releases soul-damaging traumas from this life and past lives; clears the Akashic Record of old traumas specific to being abused as a woman—rape, incest,

battering, misogyny, and repression; heals self-esteem and inner knowing; promotes pride in being a woman; encourages autonomy in women.

Emerald • *(Diaphragm)* • GREEN
Heals the purged and cleansed diaphragm chakra and emotional body; reprograms the diaphragm chakra and emotional body/Hara Line; detoxifies negativity; transforms negativity into positive emotional energy; stabilizes; soothes; offers a sense of security, harmony, and closeness to Goddess; aids understanding of one's life purpose in relation to the universal plan; aids in emotional and life-stage transitions and changes.

Epidote • *(Diaphragm)* • GREEN-BLACK
Purges and cathartically detoxifies negative emotions from the aura, once and for all cleansing of held onto and repressed emotions; opens those who have refused their spiritual growth and may not do it gently, causes drastic clearing of the emotional body aura. *Note:* Those drawn to this stone are being shaken from resistance into rapid spiritual awakening.

Erythrite • *(Causal Body Chakra)* • RED-VIOLET

Clears and opens the causal body chakra and Hara Line connection to the causal body itself; clears the spiritual and causal body auras, templates, and chakras; receives spiritual out-of-body teachers and healers, spirit guides, angels, and the Goddess; aids channeling, clairvoyance, psychic ability, and psychic knowing; fills the outer aura bodies with Light; promotes core soul healing and energy repair; heals soul fragmentation and soul damage.

Euclase • *(Throat)* • BLUE

Cleanses and purifies the throat chakra on all levels; supports throat complex repairing, rewiring, and healing; removes blockages by dissolving them; connects the levels of the throat; aids expression and creativity; helps one to speak out and release that which is "choking" or "stuck in the throat"; promotes speaking one's truth tactfully, being honest, and honoring one's inner truth; encourages positive confrontation to restore truth and balance; promotes speaking out gently.

Eudialyte • *(Causal Body Chakra)* • RED-VIOLET

Cleanses, connects, activates, and opens the causal body chakra at the base of the skull; promotes clear communication, reception, and information from the Light; develops the galactic and causal bodies (necessary for ascension and to bring in a Goddess); brings new and more advanced psychic abilities and the knowledge of how to use them; offers direct connection with Goddess and Light Be-ings; promotes spiritual evolution and ascension; supports unconditional love. *Note:* This energy is similar to that of Pink Tourmaline but on a higher level.

Feldspar • *(Belly)* • PEACH

Provides feminine, moon, and Goddess energy; aids in honoring oneself as a woman, honoring one's sexuality and ability to create new life, valuing one's body and sexuality as images of Goddess, and perceiving oneself as a Goddess; helps women who may offer their bodies too freely or to the wrong partners; promotes women's self respect and self-esteem; eases menstruation; promotes conscientious use of contraception.

Flint (Chert) • *(Belly)* • ORANGE AND BROWN

Grounds and releases anger and aggression, aids self-control, reduces a tendency to settle differences by physical or verbal abuse, reduces fighting and/or "going away mad," promotes learning to manage and safely release anger without harm to others, reduces a tendency to blame others for one's troubles and failures, aids positive self-esteem, reduces arrogance and self-righteousness.

Fluorite—Aqua • *(Throat)* • AQUA

Promotes releasing tears and expressing withheld grief and fear; aids the ability to ask others for help, healing, and comfort; supports the safe expression of anger; releases and heals anger; aids resolving fear, letting go of grief, letting go of emotional pain, and releasing the thought form that suffering is necessary in one's life.

Fluorite—Blue • *(Third Eye)* • BLUE

Reprograms the mind and mental body; accesses information from the Akashic Records; releases negative karmic patterns; rewrites karma; offers knowledge of the present life and past lives to heal their damage in the present; changes karma positively by healing the past and thereby reprogramming the present and future; provides access to the Lords of Karma, spirit guides, and angels; heals core soul fragmentation; releases negative thinking patterns.

Fluorite—Clear • *(Vision)* • CLEAR, GREY

Operates as a computer chip; promotes access to the subconscious mind, the 95 percent of the brain that is unused; obtains information and Light; aids access to the mental body grid, Earth grid, and interspace grid; promotes telepathic contact with other people, discarnate entities, spirit guides, and other-planetary Be-ings; aids communication with animals and other life forms; reprograms negative thought forms and patterns; heals subpersonalities. Use this stone as a psychic protection filter.

Fluorite—Green • *(Heart)* • GREEN

Brings mental body and mind level changes and reprogramming into the emotional body and the heart chakra, uses the mind to release emotional traumas from this lifetime, aids visualization and meditation, promotes the effectiveness of affirmations and mantras, heals heart scars, facilitates emotional release, opens the heart to understanding what happened in the past, aids in integrating multiple personalities.

Fluorite—Pink • *(Heart)* • PINK
Reprograms the mind at the astral, emotional level; heals the astral body; helps to bring the astral self/astral twin into the body; aids retrieval of soul parts; heals soul fragmentation; aids emotional integration; soothes fear and despair; promotes forgiveness of self and others, awareness of the Goddess within, trust in life, self-love, self-empowerment, emotional wholeness; support for heart dis-eases, headaches, migraines. *Note:* This stone is sometimes called Lavender Fluorite.

Fluorite—Purple • *(Crown)* • PURPLE
Provides entrance into the programming of the mind at the spiritual level, accesses spiritual information from the Light Body, makes spiritual knowledge from the outer aura body levels conscious, aids the ability to meditate, enhances psychic development, aids understanding oneself as a part

of the universal plan, promotes a sense of wholeness and spiritual peace.

Fluorite—Raspberry • *(Causal Body Chakra)* • RED-VIOLET
Reprograms the mind grid, takes mental body healing to a higher and more permanent level, removes negative programming and patterning, heals negative karmic patterns, reprograms karma, aids in healing DNA damage, reconnects full-complement DNA, promotes understanding oneself as part of a universal plan, heals the mind and brain from the spiritual body level.

Fluorite—Yellow • *(Solar Plexus)* • YELLOW
Clears mental access to the Light Body; obtains access to the mental grid; stimulates, clears, and heals all powers of the mind—intellect, visualization, psychic ability, and psychic healing; aids neurolinguistic programming, mental reprogramming, karmic release, and idea and energy assimilation of all kinds; aids uncording and removal of chakra hooks; clears attachments; heals sub-personalities and negative inner voices

Fossil • *(Grounding)* • BROWN, GREY, WHITE

All Fossils are record keepers, use for reading the ancient wisdom of the Earth; promotes ancient Earth awareness, knowledge of the soul's strength and ancient wisdom, access to the root wisdom of peoples and the planet, and knowledge of Earth and soul origins; provides awareness of the soul's individual record on this planet and individual connection to the Earth; promotes respect for age and an awareness that there is no death or end; aids grounding, serenity, peaceful aging, inner strength, and endurance.

Fossil—Ammonite • *(Earth)* • BLACK AND BROWN

The spiral and the labyrinth, fossilized reminder of life as a sacred path or journey; supports meditation, guided meditation, and path working; contacts physical and spiritual helpers along one's way—spirit guides, teachers, mothers, friends, totem animals, Goddesses, and healers; retains a pattern of one's aura and a record of one's spiritual growth if used frequently; helps one to remember where one has been and to know how, where and when to take the next step.

Fossil—Goniatite • *(Earth)* • BLACK OR BROWN AND WHITE
Connects with the Goddess on Earth and Earth Goddesses—the Goddess's spiral; promotes understanding of the cycles of life in individuals, in humankind, and in the planet; understanding the life force, life passages; aids in accepting and moving through one's own life stages from birth to death; acceptance of life, living, growth, change, dying, death

Fossil—Orthoceras • *(Earth)* • BLACK OR BROWN AND GREY
Record keeper of the stages of the Earth's growth and one's own; meditate on this stone to understand where one has been and what you have accomplished in this and past lives; provides a guidance on how to proceed next; helps in moving forward on one's path; aids decision making; aids seeing oneself and this lifetime as part of a greater plan and whole, understanding one's part in the planet's evolutionary plan.

Fossil—Rhyncholampas (Echinoids) • *(Vision)* • GREY
Magnifies our connection with the galaxy and stars; meditate on this stone to see Earth's and your own place as a member of the galaxy; keeps a record of the Milky Way—its stars and

planets, birth, growth, and movement; supports visions of the Pleiades, where the Goddess first created people in body. *Note:* These stones are fossilized starfish.

Fossil—Turritella • *(Vision)* • BROWN AND WHITE
Inspires visions of past lives, especially of past-life origins of current situations and relationships; promotes the ability to understand why people from the past are in this life now; creates an opportunity to resolve past-life relationships; heals karmic patterns; aids in ending negative past karma with significant people in this life. *Note:* These stones are made up of tiny fossilized snails.

Freshwater Pearl • *See* Pearl.

Fuchsite • *(Diaphragm)* • LIGHT GREEN
Collects emotions into the diaphragm chakra for purging and release, soothes the release process, and aids nausea; heals tears and holes in the diaphragm chakra; cleanses, purifies, and repairs; aids in karmic release. *Note:* This stone does not provide a strong healing energy alone, but it can be powerful

when found with Ruby or other gem inclusions; it can also be used with other gemstones.

Fuchsite with Kyanite • *(Thymus)* • BLUE AND GREEN
Promotes meditation on the beauty of the green Earth; supports Earth healers and others who work to restore the Earth to the garden it was created to be; promotes stewardship of the planet and its life forms, endangered species or not, supporting oneness with all life; prevents burnout; promotes peace, joy, and oneness; boosts the immune system. *Note:* Fuchsite with Kyanite is beautiful and rare.

See also Ruby with Fuchsite.

Fulgerite • *(Crown)* • SAND COLORS
Promotes transformation, breakthroughs, and enlightenment; brings the Above to the Below in the form of psychic stimulation and psychic sensory opening; puts one on a spiritual path, especially if previously uninterested in spirituality; awakens spirituality as suddenly and powerfully as a lightning bolt; promotes sudden new and transformative ideas and creativity,

transformation. and breakthroughs. *Note:* Fulgerite is also called Sand Fulgerite and is formed from lightning-struck beach sand.

Gaia Stone • *See* Obsidian—Green.

Galena (Fool's Gold) • *(Earth)* • SILVER METALLIC
For discerning truth from falsehood, reality from fantasy; balances those who tend to illusion and delusion; grounds one into earth-plane reality, promotes actively seeking what is real; traditionally used to relieve dis-eases and pain in the feet.

Garnet—Golden • *(Hara Chakra)* • YELLOW-BROWN-ORANGE
Calms, stabilizes, and centers; aids psychic development and opening with safe grounding; cleanses and repairs the hara chakra and its connections; connects the solar plexus chakra to the Hara Line; gives power to any psychic work; aids distance healing, visualization, energy transmission, and psychic communication; stabilizes and promotes the development and manifestation of one's life purpose. *Note:* Golden Garnet is usually Hessionite Garnet.

Garnet—Green (Demantoid) • *(Heart)* • EMERALD GREEN

Draws prosperity, abundance, money, success, and luck; promotes growth and increase of all kinds—gardens, ideas, or bank accounts; heals the heart of present and past poverty and residual poverty consciousness; promotes manifesting or obtaining what one needs; aids knowing the difference between what one needs and what one wants; helps to exchange materialism for spiritual peace; promotes abundance from within. Note: Demantoid Green Garnet is sometimes confused with Grossularite Garnet, which is yellow-green rather than bright emerald green. Demantoid Garnet has different uses and is the most expensive of the Garnets.

Garnet—Orange • *(Belly)* • LIGHT ORANGE

Stabilizes physical and nonphysical energy; detoxifies, cleanses, and purifies; insulates the aura and auric field from energy damage and overload; repairs holes and tears in the aura; balances the aura's magnetic field; protects the connections between mind and body; heals emotional damage; supports fertility, reproduction, pregnancy, and childbirth; helps in recovery from rape and sexual abuse. *Note:* This form of Orange Garnet is also called Spessartite.

Garnet—Raspberry • *(Perineum)* • PINK-RED

Connects the Hara and Kundalini Lines at the root and perineum chakras; aids in bringing life force energy from the Earth into the body through the Kundalini and Hara Lines; stimulates sexuality and promotes fertility, conception, and orgasm; heals the vagina, uterus, and ovaries; repels negativity and disharmonious others. *Note:* Also called Rhodolite or Almandine Garnet, this stone is not to be confused with Rubellite Tourmaline.

Garnet—Red • *(Root)* • RED

Promotes root chakra opening; warms, grounds, and directs kundalini energy into the root center; draws Earth energy into the body; stimulates the life force; aids accepting and balancing this incarnation; promotes sexuality and fertility; repels disharmonious individuals from one's aura energy—sometimes drastically and decisively; brings out anger and sexual attraction; draws your harmonious and sexually compatible mate; aids sexual healing and tantric sex; promotes a monogamous and stable marriage with same- or opposite-sex true lovers. *Note:* This is usually Pyrope Garnet.

Garnet—Yellow-Green (Grossularite)
(Solar Plexus) • YELLOW-GREEN
Cleanses the solar plexus and heart chakras; detoxifies the Kundalini Line; clears the effects of negative emotions like envy, anger, greed, jealousy, and vengefulness; diffuses negative emotions; highlights the part of the body affected by harboring negative emotions; cleanses the negative to bring in the positive; promotes unconditional love and inner peace once one learns the relevant lesson, promotes forgiveness of others and oneself.

Gaspaite • *(Movement)* • BROWN AND GREEN
Aids moving forward on one's life path, removes blocks, heals and repairs, removes hesitation and self-consciousness, promotes self-confidence and certainty of oneself and one's path, eases the fear of moving forward, promotes positive change and spiritual evolution, promotes emotional growth, supports soul growth.

Gel Lithium Silica • *(Causal Body Chakra)* • RED-VIOLET
Calms, stabilizes, and balances; eases stress; promotes and

supports unconditional love; promotes connection with the Light, feeling the Light's love in every aspect of one's life; encourages awareness of constantly being loved and cared for; aids acceptance; heals grief and loss, heartache, heartbreak, and loneliness.

Gem Silica • *(Thymus)* • AQUA
Clears the energies of sexual, emotional, and physical abuse from the emotional body; heals trauma from present-life and past life; prevents present-life traumas from becoming karmic patterns; heals past-life karmic patterns of abuse; promotes connection with Goddess and the angelic realm; promotes self-empowerment, joy in being a woman, and women's all-healing. *Note:* This is the crystalline form of Chrysocolla.

Goethite • *(Earth)* • BLACK
Takes one deep into the core of the planet or the core of one's own Be-ing; stimulates stability, safety, security, and stillness within; calms; aids connection with the Earth, with planetary origins, and with one's own herstory on the planet; opens access to karmic information and healing;

promotes being present on the earth-plane and fully engaged in fulfilling the requirements of this incarnation; promotes inner certainty.

Gold • *(Solar Plexus)* • METALLIC GOLD
Clears and opens the chakras of the mental body; aids intellect, clear thought, spatial perspective, and rationality; stimulates positive aggressiveness and initiative; promotes mechanical, electrical, technical, and computer awareness; aids psychic openness; promotes psychic and mental analysis without emotion; clears the energy channel from the solar plexus to the third eye chakra; builds the immune system according to traditional use; provides masculine energy.

Goldstone—Blue • *(None)* • BLUE
Goldstone is a man-made ceramic. Though some healers believe it has metaphysical properties, I do not.

Goldstone—Red • *(None)* • RED
Goldstone is a man-made ceramic. Though some healers believe it has metaphysical properties, I do not.

Goshenite (Clear Beryl) • *(Vision)* • CLEAR

Aids the ability to see and clear old patterns and pain, supports karmic healing, promotes visioning past-life traumas to release and heal them, reprograms karma through understanding past-life pain manifested in this lifetime, eases fear of karmic "seeing" and of reexperiencing the past, aids understanding of old patterns and filling in the missing pieces of information, completes karmic information and clearing, fills the soul with Light and hope, promotes karmic grace.

Halite (Salt)—Blue • *(Third Eye)* • BLUE

Disinfects the third eye and all the kundalini chakras and channels of negative energy, attachments, entities, spirit possessions, and psychic attacks; removes negative influences from one's psychic perceptions and psychic senses, especially from clairvoyance; clears blocks to one's psychic opening, development, or abilities; heals a distorted sense of reality on the mental and psychic levels. *Note:* Halite draws negativity into itself and must be cleared frequently in sunlight (not water) to release it.

Halite (Salt)—Clear • *(Transpersonal Point)* • CLEAR AND WHITE
Disinfects the aura of negative energy—negative thought forms, entities, and attachments; repels and removes negativity; provides protection from negative entities, psychic attacks, and possessions; aids in changing negative thought patterns and bad habits to positive ones; protects alcohol drinkers from bringing home bar attachments. *Note:* Halite draws negativity into itself and must be cleared frequently in sunlight (not water) to release it.

Halite (Salt)—Pink • *(Crown)* • PINK AND LAVENDER
Disinfects the crown and all the kundalini chakras and channels from negative energy, entities, spirit possessions, and attachments; repels and removes negativity from one's spiritual outlook; clears blocks to one's spiritual opening or development; clears blocks from one's psychic abilities; protects alcohol drinkers from bringing home bar attachments. *Note:* Halite draws negativity into itself and must be cleared frequently in sunlight (not water) to release it.

Hanksite • *(Solar Plexus)* • GOLD

Promotes understanding the truth of what you see; promotes discernment, reduces gullibility; aids awareness of bad contracts, fraud, illusions, lies, delusions, bad deals, and being cheated; prevents being "sold the Brooklyn bridge"; helps in being truthful to others; helps in seeing oneself and others as part of the Goddess and in respecting the sacredness of each; offers protection from trickster/coyote energy; supports recovery from gambling addictions. *Note:* Do not clear this stone in water; it will dissolve.

Hawk's Eye • *(Vision)* • BLACK AND SILVER

Increases a psychic's ability to see what is wrong and then change it, transforms negative energy into positive, heals negative energy brought in from past lives, promotes the ability to see and release karmic attachments and negative entities from the aura, clears and grounds negative energy from the Hara Line; aids the ability to see and clear hara chakra hooks, traditionally used to increase night vision and psychic vision. *Note:* Hawk's Eye is Black Tiger Eye. *See also* Tiger Eye—Black or Blue.

Healer's Gold • *See* Apache Gold.

Hemalyke • *(None)* • METALLIC BLACK
Hemalyke is not a gemstone but the trade name for a synthetic form of Hematite. Sometimes made magnetic, there are no healing properties to the stone itself, though there may be in the added magnetism.

Hematite • *(Earth)* • BLACK OVER RED
Grounds and stabilizes one's incarnation into the earth-plane, heals karmic anger and rage, heals those who were warriors in past lives and in this life, promotes courage in facing karmic battles, provides courage in wartime or childbirth, promotes facing and healing one's shadow side, fosters peace and nonaggression, stops bleeding and hemorrhaging according to tradition, prevents excessive bleeding in childbirth, eases menstrual flooding.

Hematite—Magnetic • *(Root)* • METALLIC BLACK
Balances and stimulates the magnetic energies of the aura and auric field, promotes grounding but in a dynamic way,

heals the magnetic properties and polarities of the energy system; playing with these magnets activates the healing. *Note:* These stones are made in China of reconstituted Hematite and then are magnetized; they are usually sold in pairs and are the newest metaphysical toy fad. The magnetism is fairly strong—keep them away from watches and computers.

Hemimorphite—Aqua • *(Thymus)* • AQUA
Returns joy to one's life, promotes emotional ease and a sense of well-being, reduces emotional and physical pain, reduces bone pain, supports lung healing, helps to stop smoking, detoxifies gently, clears and detoxifies the Hara Line and emotional body, heals and merges-in the astral body twin, helps to bring in one's Higher Self and to clear the Light Body, promotes spiritual evolution and all ascension processes.

Hemimorphite—White • *(Crown)* • WHITE
Promotes healing for the brain, aids the ability to use more than the usual 5 percent of the brain, balances right- and left-brain hemispheres, aids dyslexics who try to use both sides of the brain at once, helps in sorting and sequencing

information and impressions, promotes understanding of psychic impressions and information, supports and aids vision on all levels.

Herderite • *(Third Eye)* • WHITE
Promotes expansion of consciousness, altered states, awareness of simultaneous realities, and awareness of past lives; aids expansion of psychic abilities, multidimensional travel, astral travel, clairvoyance (psychic sight), and visions; promotes awareness of planes of existence beyond the physical; offers protection while traveling out of body; promotes understanding of what is psychically perceived; expands and repairs the auric field.

Herkimer Diamond • *(Transpersonal Point)* • CLEAR
Provides the energy of pure love and pure information and Light; facilitates gentle transformation; promotes harmony within, with others, and with one's world; aids fine-tuning of aura energy and of the etheric, emotional, mental, and spiritual bodies; aligns the physical and spiritual self; promotes mental clarity, expansion of awareness, and positivity; promotes the

feeling of having everything one needs; aids living in the present peacefully; connects to other dimensions and the stars; connects the individual to the Light grid and to one's Light Body and Oversoul (Goddess Self); aids soul retrieval; draws one's soul mate and soul friends; stimulates core soul healing; provides very comforting energy.

Heulandite • *(Third Eye)* • WHITE
Programs the mental body for the ability to create one's own reality, provides entrance into the Void—the creative mental source of all existence; promotes understanding that all limits are in the mind, heals the mind and releases limitations, supports the ability to manifest a good life.

Hiddenite (Green Kunzite) • *(Diaphragm)* • LIME GREEN
Detoxifies the physical body of emotional pain; heals dis-ease resulting from repressed emotions in this and past lives; aids one's ability to feel emotions; releases fear; promotes compassion for others and reaching out to others; aids self-awareness, discernment, letting go, and trust in Goddess. *See also* Kunzite.

Hole-y Stone • *(Grounding)* • BROWN

Presents a keyhole psychic link with nature realms—look through the hole to see fairies, devas, leprechauns, elves, sprites, water spirits, and pixies; provides a new view of the small lives on Earth; promotes compassion for and communication with animals, plants, insects, birds, and reptiles; promotes respect for the oneness of all life.

Howlite • *(Vision)* • WHITE AND GREY

Creates and unmasks delusion and illusion in one's life, creates and exposes masks and costumes on the mental level, exposes occasions of deluding oneself and others, creates and tears down realities, refuses one truth to create another, creates a positive or a negative escape for oneself, can be used honestly or dishonestly toward others; expands consciousness, expands limitations. *Note:* This is the natural form of the stone. Howlite is commercially dyed in many colors to imitate Turquoise and other gemstones.

Idocrase • *See* Vesuvianite.

Indian Paint Stone • *See* Paint Stone.

Indicolite • *See* Tourmaline—Blue.

Iolite (Water Sapphire) • *(Third Eye)* • INDIGO
Opens, heightens, and expands psychic abilities in a gentle way; teaches the parameters of one's psychic abilities and possibilities; good for those of strong potential who are new on the spiritual path; encourages and protects psychic exploration; enhances curiosity and achievement; guides one through spiritual beginnings and growth. Useful for people who are new to spiritual opening.

Itacolumite (Flexible Sandstone) • *(Movement)* • GREY AND TAN
Aids the ability to move forward on one's path; eases resistance and rigidity; promotes flexibility of outlook, adaptability, and the ability to flow with life and change; reduces fear of change and movement; offers courage, grounding, and the ability to bend with the wind; provides emotional support for sufferers of hip, knee, leg, and foot dis-eases.

Ivory (Bone) • *(Third Eye)* • WHITE, BEIGE

Promotes recognition of Earth's ancientness, respect for all species, thanks for what the animals have given us to sustain and enhance human lives, awareness of extinct and endangered species, and respect for the oneness of all life; encourages nurturing and supporting other people and animals and receiving the same for oneself; honors the planet's abundance and living beauty.

Jade—African • *See* Jasper—Green.

Jade—Black • *(Earth)* • BLACK

Promotes coming fully into this incarnation for the purpose of enlightenment; for understanding and healing karma; aids ego nonattachment; fosters peace on Earth and in oneself, promotes Earth healing and environmental awareness, encourages compassion for other-than-human lives on Earth—animals, plants, insects, birds; aids communication with animals and nonhuman life forms; promotes respect for the oneness of all life.

Jade—Green (True Jade) • *(Heart)* • DARK GREEN

Opens the qualities of mercy and compassion for all sentient Be-ings, promotes oneness with all that lives; aids heart opening and heart healing; frees one from anger, selfishness, and greed; supports service to others and the planet; aids bodhisattvas and those on the path of enlightenment, providing Kwan Yin energy; soothes the emotions; aids movement on one's life path, fosters trust in the Goddess; promotes calm acceptance of the suffering in life; aids one's ability to be giving to others; supports healing for the hips and kidneys. *Note:* This stone is also called Nephrite or Nephrite Jade—it is becoming very rare. *See* Serpentine Jade for other varieties.

Jade—Lemurian • *(Root)* • BLACK AND GOLD

Raises the vibration of the physical, or etheric, body; brings in the Light to evolve and uplift the physical Be-ing; provides connection with the Earth and the Well of Life; aids connection of above with below; stabilizes the life force and this incarnation; keeps one in the body without shutting out divine guidance; offers protection and insulation of the energy channels; invites the participation of angels in one's daily life; reminds us that we are spiritual Be-ings. *Note:* Lemurian Jade is the New Age name for Jade mixed with Pyrite.

Jade—Malaysia • *(None)* • ANY COLORS

Commercial name for a stone that is not Jade but is instead dyed Quartz.

Jade—Mountain • *(None)* • ANY COLORS

Commercial name for a stone that is not Jade but is instead dyed Dolomite or Marble.

Jade—Pink • *(Heart)* • PINK OR PEACH

Opens one's heart to all sentient Be-ings including oneself; promotes compassion for the suffering of all life; promotes taking the Bodhisattva Vow; supports bodhisattvas incarnated on Earth, aids all who are in service to others and the planet; heals the heart and emotions of grief, heartache and disappointment; aids healers' burnout and despair; promotes acceptance and unconditional love.

Jade—Purple • *(Crown)* • LAVENDER

Awakens spirituality; develops and opens the crown chakra; works slowly to prevent overload; eases fear of psychic or spiritual opening; puts one on a spiritual path; opens psychic abilities and teaches one how to use them; aids in understanding and clearing one's karma and in working with the Lords of Karma; traditionally used for luck, good fortune, peace, health, prosperity, and protection from misfortune and accidents. *Note:* Colors range from pale almost-pink to very dark purple; be aware that much of the Purple Jade sold commercially is dyed.

Jade—White • *(Third Eye)* • WHITE

Promotes healing and positively programming the mind and brain, stimulates brain function and using more of one's brain power; reduces overwhelm in those awakening spiritually, supports adaptation to new abilities; aids dream work and prophetic dreams, raises consciousness gently and safely; awakens spirituality; calms, relaxes, eases insomnia. Recommended for people opening psychically, as it stabilizes, calms, and helps to open slowly.

Jade—Yellow • *(Solar Plexus)* • YELLOW
Supports the Buddhist path to enlightenment and all other spiritual paths; aids meditation and visualization; teaches nonattachment; helps in overcoming ego, selfishness and greed; stimulates and heals the mental body; promotes heightened awareness and compassion; aids the understanding that enlightenment only happens while incarnated, promotes respect for the body; promotes a peaceful mind; calms, reduces stress; soothes the digestive and urinary systems.

Note: There are many kinds and types of Jaspers and the same stone can carry a variety of different names within the larger Jasper category. There is no standardization for these names, and I have done my best to name the varieties with as much accuracy as possible.

Jasper—Bloodstone • *See* Bloodstone.

Jasper—Brown • *(Hara Chakra)* • BROWN AND ORANGE
Protects and repairs the etheric double aura's energy envelope; heals aura tears from trauma, anesthetics, prescription

or recreational drugs, alcohol use, fear, physical pain, or psychic attack; helps to retain aura integrity against negative energy and others' negative thought forms; helps to filter out the negative mass consciousness; helps to delineate boundaries between oneself and others.

Jasper—Bulico • *(Root)* • RED, BROWN AND WHITE

Supports menopause, balances menstrual and hormonal irregularities, aids heavy menstrual flow, aids recovery from hysterectomy—encouraging rebalancing and feeling well, supports women who fear that menopause means a loss of their femininity or feminine identity, helps in dealing with and accepting one's changing body; grounds, stabilizes, and comforts.

Jasper—Cobra • *(Movement)* • TAN AND WHITE

Aids forward movement on one's life path, protects one's tentative first steps toward spiritual growth emotionally, aids a baby's first steps physically, protects those new to spirituality; helps balance psychic opening, grounds change and transformation in the body, promotes courage in stepping out and stepping forward, offers the courage to grow and change.

Jasper—Crazy Lace • *(Hara Chakra)* • GOLD AND TAN
Helps to establish one's life purpose; aids knowing what one's life purpose is and how to proceed with it; promotes being certain of one's path, aids choosing among possibilities, feeling stable on one's life path, and knowing you can handle it; supports people who don't know their path, wish to change careers, and for those who want to make their career their life purpose.

Jasper—Dalmatian • *(Root)* • BLACK AND OFF-WHITE
Brings one back to Earth; turns off psychic awareness for focus on earth-plane life; reduces or stops being overwhelmed by psychic input; shuts off psychic impressions without shutting out the Light; protects against bad dreams, prevents astral travel; aids grounding and filtering; protects from negative energies and low-level entities. *Note:* This is not a strong protective or healing energy.

Jasper—Fancy • *See* Ocean Jasper.

Jasper—Flower • *See* Ocean Jasper.

Blue Labradorite
Fushite
Polished Amethyst
Natural Citrine Points

Creedite

Kunzite

Optical Clear Calcite

Tourmaline on Smoky Quartz

Blue Fluorite with Iron

Purple, Clear, and Green Fluorite

Turquoise

Red Garnet

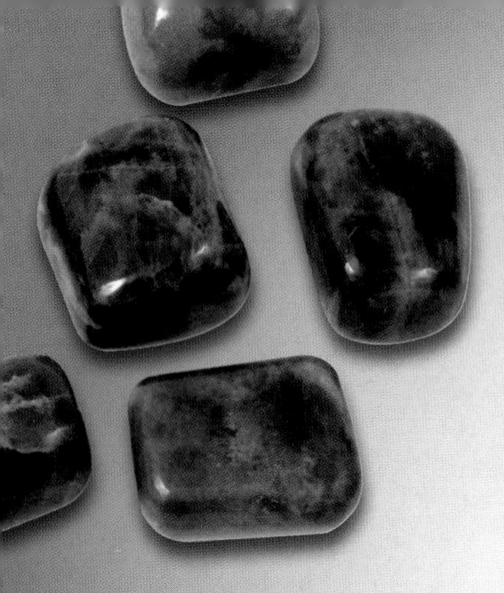

Green Vesuvianite

Obsidian

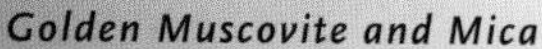

Golden Muscovite and Mica

Double Terminated Quartz with Iron

Citrine

Red Calcite

Smoky Quartz

Calcite

Pyrite

Amazonite

Cobalt Blue Obsidian

Azurite and Chrysocolla

Quartz with Pyrite and Galena

Scolecite with Quartz

Amethyst with Calcite

Rose Quartz

Green Calcite

Selenite Desert Rose

Jasper—Fossil • *(Hara Chakra)* • RED-BROWN
All fossils are record keepers; contains a record of all of one's incarnations, how one's life purpose continues from lifetime to lifetime and how it manifests in different incarnations; promotes understanding of one's life purpose and soul purpose; aids understanding of one's place in life and the greater plan; promotes service to the Light; helps in manifesting one's life path and purpose; promotes understanding the nature of one's soul; promotes soul growth.

Jasper—Golden Lace • *(Hara Chakra)* • BROWN AND ORANGE
Opens conscious knowledge of the living library, encodes the herstory of all peoples that came to colonize Earth and the planets they came from, encodes the herstory and origins of all species brought to Earth and developed here, encodes the herstory of life on Earth since other-planetary arrival, contains the keys to the future development of Earth peoples and species, promotes full-complement DNA connection and healing, protects people who work with the living library, accesses information and the Light. *Note:* Golden Lace Jasper (or Agate) was formerly known as

Chinese Writing Rock; however, Chinese Writing Rock in this book is a different gemstone.

Jasper—Green • *(Solar Plexus)* • GREEN
Provides peace, luck, prosperity and good fortune, inner growth, and inner peace; offers acceptance of change; promotes slow but steady evolution and soul growth; encourages gentle progressive change; aids adaptability; increases one's ability to manifest abundance in one's life—financial and more; heals anger and poverty; supports the kidneys and kidney healing. *Note:* This stone is also commercially known as African Jade. *See also* Bloodstone, which is Green and Red Jasper, and Kambaba Jasper, which is green and black.

Jasper—Indio • *(Grounding)* • BROWN AND BLUE
Brings the Light into physical form; brings Light healing into the body from higher levels and Be-ings; promotes grounding; works with the grounding channels rather than the chakras; aids Light Be-ings in their work of healing people, animals, and the Earth by enhancing their ability to make and hold physical contact with those they are healing; promotes

stability, comfort, and calming; reduces nausea and dizziness. *Note:* Also called Indian Jasper, this stone combines Jasper with veins of Chalcedony or Agate.

Jasper—Kambaba • *(Heart)* • GREEN AND BLACK

Looks deep into one's own and others' hearts; promotes soul searching, finding oneself, self-analysis, and seeing who others really are; finds the inner truth about oneself and one's life; finds the inner truth about others; helps in seeing oneself and others with compassion; promotes unconditional love for others and oneself; aids self-acceptance and self-respect; promotes rethinking and change in one's life.

Jasper—Leopard Skin • *(Grounding)* • BROWN AND TAN

Offers protection as one manifests one's path; protects one while fulfilling one's life purpose and karmic agreements on the earth-plane; promotes help along the path; provides safety and security in achieving life goals; aids grounding in daily life and work; helps to turn one's life work into one's daily occupation or job; promotes grounding, concentration, and stabilization; aids the ability to focus.

Jasper—Mookite • *(Belly)* • RED AND YELLOW
The colors and energies work together to balance and heal the belly; eases menstrual cramps, promotes menstrual flow, balances women's hormones, eases menopause symptoms and emotions, brings the emotions and hormones into balance. *Note:* Mookite is red and yellow Jasper found separate or blended in nature; it is often strung as beads or chips.

Jasper—Mountain Blue • *(Throat)* • BLUE AND GREY
Promotes receptivity on all levels; clears, heals, regenerates and opens the throat chakra and throat complex; aids the ability to put ideas into words; aids conceptualization, visualization, perception, and comprehension; promotes the creation and manifestation of thought; promotes the ability to describe one's inner reality; aids psychic reception, telepathy, and empathy; aids psychic communication with people, animals, and nature spirits; calms and soothes. *Note:* Mountain Blue Jasper is similar in energy and appearance to Montana Agate.

Jasper—Ocean • *(Entire Kundalini Line)* • ALL COLORS
Stabilizes and balances the entire Kundalini Line and the physical, etheric, and emotional bodies; aligns, repairs, and opens the chakras and the auric field; provides a sense of calm, wellness, well-being, grounding, and wholeness. *Note:* A string of Ocean Jasper beads will have all the chakra colors in it, and it aids the physical and emotional bodies as a whole unit. This Jasper is also called Flower or Fancy Jasper.

Jasper—Ocean Wave • *(Thymus)* • BLUE-GREEN
Supports pregnancy and childbirth, breast-feeding, infant protection, and caretaking; promotes honoring the mystery of gestation and birth, new lives; aids new mothers and mothers-to-be emotionally; supports women with morning sickness. Use this stone for issues dealing with the beginnings of life, as it represents the watery depths of the ocean and the element of water—saltwater.

Jasper—Picture • *(Vision)* • GREEN, GREY AND TAN
Stimulates visualization of this life and past-life scenes, promotes visions from lifetimes on other planets, promotes awareness of

the beauty of the Earth, aids the ability to visualize and meditate, supports and stabilizes creativity and new ideas for visual artists; opens artists' block, aids drawing and painting.

Jasper—Poppy • *(Movement)* • PINK AND TAN
Protects the etheric aura, repairs tears and breaks in the etheric aura and etheric body, helps one stay on one's path and move forward, protects from obstructions, promotes clarity in oneself and compassion for others, provides a protective filter against other people's negativity about one's life, filters the negative mass consciousness. aids in maintaining clear boundaries between oneself and others.

Jasper—Rainforest • *(Heart)* • BROWN AND GREEN
Shaman's stone for connection with nature, plants, animals, forests, saving the rainforest and the Earth; promotes contact with devas, nature spirits, wildlife, Earth Goddesses, and the planet herself; aids shamans, herbalists, animal healers and communicators, planetary activists, and rainforest activists; reminds one to "love your Mother" and help her heal and survive; supports advocating

for our Mother the Earth. *Note:* Rainforest Jasper is also known as Rhyolite.

Jasper—Red • *(Belly)* • RED ORANGE

Balances anger and sexuality, heals women's anger at men; calms men's sexual aggressiveness toward women; helps balance physical sexuality with emotions in gay and heterosexual relationships; promotes sexual compatibility and tantric sex between lovers; helps to balance irregular menstrual cycles, ovulation, and menstrual cramps; brings on menstruation

Jasper—Red-Banded • *(Belly)* • RED, ORANGE, WHITE

Provides emotional support for most women's sexuality and reproductive issues; promotes menstruation; eases menstrual cramps; supports first sexual experiences in young women and men; heals fear of one's sexuality, fear of love-making, confusion about one's sexual orientation, fear of being gay, fear of being different, and coming out; supports adolescents who are learning who they are sexually, whether they are heterosexual or homosexual. *Note:* Red-Banded Jasper is sometimes erroneously called Red Malachite.

Jasper—Royal Imperial • *(Belly)* • RED-BROWN

Supports sexuality, fertility, pregnancy, easy labor, and safe delivery; nurtures and welcomes a coming child; sends the message that a child is wanted and loved; charms against miscarriage and postpartum depression; supports breast-feeding and promotes breast milk after delivery; use as an overall women's fertility charm and good luck stone. *Note:* The pattern of inclusions in this Jasper looks like a fetus in the womb.

Jasper—Silver Leaf • *(Entire Kundalini Line)* • TAN AND GREY

Grounds the Kundalini Line channels and system into the core of the Earth; provides stability, calm, centering, and grounding; aids physical and emotional balance; provides a sense of wellness and solidity; promotes a sense of knowing one's place in life; promotes being rooted; supports planetary meditation and Earth healing work.

Jasper—Snakeskin • *(Root)* • BLACK AND BROWN

Grounds, promotes the ability to be centered and rooted, aids one in being a part of the Earth, enhances the ability to "come back down to Earth" quickly after psychic work or channeling, aids spaciness, brings one back to present time; this stone can be too grounding for those who wish full use of their psychic abilities; use in moderation.

Jasper—Spiderweb • *(Root)* • RED-BROWN

Stabilizes, reduces and heals phobias and fears, provides centered grounding, repairs the entire grounding system, repairs the root chakra, provides healing energy for women who have been raped or violated, supports those unsure of their sexuality, aids gays in "coming out," aids in taking pride in who one is. *Note:* This stone is found in shades of brown with red circular inclusions, and in black with red lines and striations.

Jasper—Stefoinite • *(Entire Hara Line)* • BROWN AND BLUE

Channels energy; brings in Earth energy from the feet to the head through the Hara Line; aids the flow of Earth energy; promotes one's ability to learn Earth wisdom; encourages affinity for the plant, rock, and fairy realms; represents the element of Earth; promotes grounding, stabilizes stewards in care of the Earth and Earth life forms.

Jasper—Yellow • *(Movement)* • YELLOW-TAN
Protects and repairs the etheric double aura from the groin area down—thighs, legs, knees, and feet; protects movement on one's life path when it is vulnerable to distraction and scattering; aids people who are accident prone or clumsy. *Note:* This is not a strong healing energy, but it is useful for some people, and especially good for children.

For other Jaspers, *see also* Bloodstone, Mugglestone, and Wonderstone.

Jet • *(Earth)* • BLACK
Helps to heal the grief of losing one's place among the stars; heals the longing for one's soul's home; supports accepting the limits of incarnation and the physical body; aids accepting the Earth as where one needs to be for the present; opens ancient wisdom, the souls' wisdom, the wisdom of the body, and the wisdom of the planet; gemstone of the Wiccan Horned God.

Kammererite • *(Crown)* • PURPLE
Puts one on a spiritual path; causes forceful psychic opening

that may not be comfortable and may frighten beginners; cleanses, purifies, repairs, detoxifies, connects, rewires, and reprograms the crown chakra, crown system, and Kundalini Line; opens the templates to bring one's Spirit into the body; provides energy for advanced healers and psychics on the ascension path, too intense for most beginners.

Kinoite • *(Throat)* • BLUE
Clears the throat of negative speech; aids thinking, feeling, and speaking in positive ways; reprograms the etheric template and etheric body level to heal karmic misalignments and wrong programming; heals DNA, the mental body, and the mind grid; supports people with mental disabilities, stimulates those with normal abilities to higher levels of growth; eases genetic throat dis-eases and throat cancers.

Kornerupine • *(Heart)* • DARK GREEN
Brings calm and balance into one's life, grounds the overuse of psychic energy, heals the emotional heart, clears heart scars; provides emotional support for blood circulation and red blood cell production, supports heart rhythm, balances

personal biorhythms; brings the Goddess of Compassion into one's life, encourages compassion for oneself and others. *Note:* The energy of this stone is similar to that of True Jade.

Kunzite—Blue • *(Causal Body Chakra)* • BLUE-VIOLET

Heals and balances the causal body chakra; aids in receiving healing energy from spirit guides, angels, other-planetary helpers, and Pleiadian healers; aids in core soul and outer energy body repair; promotes alignment and healing; aids in bringing in one's Higher Self, promotes the ascension process; clears karmic debts, aids karmic release work; aids clear channeling and the ability to hold and balance strong psychic energy; calms.

Kunzite—Clear • *(Transpersonal Point)* • CLEAR

Heals core soul damage, damage from past lives, and soul fragmentation; aids soul retrieval, emotional body healing, energy alignment, and balance; promotes astral (higher emotional body) healing, brings the astral body twin into the physical aura; promotes the resolution of karma.

Kunzite—Green • *See* Hiddenite.

Kunzite—Pink • *(Heart)* • PINK AND LAVENDER

Provides calm, balance, stability, peace, and compassion; aids the ability to open one's heart to trust and love; protects vulnerability; heals negativity in oneself; heals effects of other people's negativity caused by fear and insecurity; connects and clears the heart, throat, third eye, and crown chakras; opens self-protecting blocks in the kundalini chakras from past emotional pain and trauma; opens the heart's ability to give, forgive and receive; heals emotions and the emotional body; aids working with spirit guides for healing and self-healing; promotes trust in the Goddess and oneself.

Kunzite—Purple • *(Crown)* • PURPLE

Aids contact with angels, spirit guides, Light Be-ings, and the Lords of Karma; brings the violet flame of purification, harmony and spiritual growth into the aura; promotes a life of spiritual awareness and opening; creates balance between present and past lives; provides all-aura healing and protection, psychic clearing, and protection from psychic attack and negative energy; fosters karmic release and healing, core soul healing, and emotional body healing; promotes safety, security, inner peace, and trust in the Goddess; helps all healing processes on every level.

Kyanite—Aqua • *(Thymus)* • AQUA
Opens, clears, and balances the thymus chakra; connects the emotional body, the Hara Line, to the etheric body, the Kundalini Line; enables one to process feelings and release sorrow, alienation, anger, and grief; promotes compassion for the suffering and oneness of all life, compassion for oneself, forgiveness and self-forgiveness; aids the ability to reach out to others and to love again after loss.

Kyanite—Black • *(Earth)* • BLACK
Roots the current incarnation into the earth-plane, opens and balances the Hara Line chakras and channels; opens one's intergalactic and interplanetary heritage as an Earth Be-ing in this lifetime; fosters awareness of Earth stewardship; aids contact with other-planetary helpers; promotes understanding of the immortality of the soul and the between-life

state; aids meditation, past-life regression work, future-life progression, and meditation between lives; grounds, calms, and centers.

Kyanite—Blue • *(Causal Body Chakra)* • SILVER–BLUE
Connects the Kundalini and Hara Line channels at the thymus; balances, aligns, opens, expands, and heals Kundalini and Hara energy channels and chakras; heals blockages and burnout from all aura bodies—etheric, emotional, mental, and spiritual; supports the healing of throat dis-eases and blockages; aids communication physically and psychically; promotes telepathy and empathy with spirit guides, angels, discarnate Be-ings, pets, extraterrestrials, and Light Be-ings; aids manifesting one's life work on the earth-plane; boosts the immune system.

Kyanite—Brown • *(Hara Chakra)* • ORANGE-BROWN
Opens and expands the hara chakra and entire Hara Line, balances energy, stabilizes and aids one's life purpose, promotes understanding and manifesting one's life purpose and life agreements on the earth-plane, stimulates and increases

the Ch'i kung microcosmic orbit, boosts and stabilizes the life force, promotes all-balancing and all-healing.

Kyanite with Rubellite

(Causal Body Chakra) • BLUE AND RED-VIOLET

Opens and balances the causal body chakra, opens and balances all the Hara Line chakras and channels, brings spiritual and soul level information to bear upon one's life purpose and path, promotes manifesting one's life purpose on the earth-plane, provides calm and confidence in one's life and life work, promotes certainty of the way, spiritualizes one's life, repairs full-complement DNA, aids those on the bodhisattva path, aids achieving one's full potential. *Note:* This is an important new gemstone energy.

Labradorite—Blue • *(Third Eye)* • INDIGO

Stimulates the third eye chakra for psychic awareness of other dimensions, promotes contact with other-planetary and other-dimensional healing and helpers and protects from negative Be-ings and interference, promotes contact with angels and the universal mind grid, aids contact with the Lords of Karma for healing past lives and the present lifetime, aids realization and karmic awareness, purifies and heals the mental body and universal mental grid.

Labradorite—Golden • *(Solar Plexus)* • YELLOW AND GOLD

Heals will, concentration, courage, and clarity; promotes taking one's freedom; heals those who subject themselves to others' manipulation and those who manipulate others; reduces codependency and co-alcoholism; fills the etheric double, emotional body aura, and mental body aura with Light; opens and heals the mental body and Light Body; promotes connection with the mental grid and Earth grid; heals confusion and indecision.

Labradorite—Grey • *(Vision)* • SILVER-GREY

Connects the emotional and mental bodies to one's life purpose and physical action; activates the Hara Line; protects and clears the aura of negative energy, psychic attacks, negative alien interference and implants, attachments, and spirit possessions; opens the vision chakras for using the eyes as lasers in psychic healing; promotes the ability to use a pendulum accurately; increases psychic vision and visualization; aids the ability to see and communicate with positive other-planetary Be-ings; promotes consciousness of one's life purpose.

Labradorite—White • *See* Moonstone—Rainbow.

Lake Michigan Concretion • *(Grounding)* • BROWN
Roots one into the Earth; promotes knowing the Goddess as the Earth herself, knowing the Goddess's support and nurturing; promotes awareness of having everything one needs for an abundant life; promotes a sense of security and safety, knowing oneself taken care of on the Goddess Earth; supports fertility and creativity; grounds. *Note:* These stone formations are natural Goddess images of an ancient type.

Lapis Lazuli • *(Throat and Third Eye)* • BLUE
Cleanses the mental body, provides deep penetration to heal outdated thought forms and mental patterns, prevents negative thoughts from becoming karmic patterns, releases outworn karmic patterns for healing, changes negative views of reality to positive outlooks, heals mental body damage from old traumas

in this life, reprograms the mental body, provides a powerful all-healing energy. *Note:* Lapis is best worn with other stones like Amethyst or Rose Quartz to gentle its forceful effects.

Larimar • *(Throat)* • BLUE AND WHITE
Helps soul mates to find and recognize each other; heals negative karma between soul mates and lovers; opens honest communication between soul mates; promotes speaking and listening with awareness, putting the other and the relationship first; stabilizes new relationships between soul mates; offers calm certainty; opens creativity and the throat chakra. Note: Larimar comes from a single mine in the Dominican Republic; it is becoming increasingly rare and expensive. *Note:* Also called Pectolite or Dolphin Stone.

Larvikite • *(Transpersonal Point)* • IRIDESCENT GREY
Accesses past lives, releases karmic patterns and their sources, works with the Lords of Karma and Divine Director, aids access to one's own Akashic Records and that of others, stimulates visual images of the karmic origins of current suffering and aids in their release and resolution; promotes

healing the present by looking at the past, promotes ascension. *Note:* Larvikite resembles Labradorite visually, but its energy is more similar to Phantom Quartz. The stone is considered magickal in Scandinavia where it is mined.

Lazulite • *(Throat)* • DARK BLUE
Clears the throat of things one couldn't say; aids in speaking out, speaking one's truth, and releasing what can't be said aloud; opens the throat for creativity; aids in healing and opening the templates between energy bodies; aids in receiving channeled information, promotes telepathic sending and receiving.

Lepidolite • *(Crown)* • LAVENDER AND PINK
Connects the heart and crown chakras to bring spiritual understanding to suffering and pain; aids in understanding the purpose of heart pain and the growth brought by suffering; promotes understanding one's life purpose and place in the universal plan; opens and releases pain and suffering layer by layer; releases karmic suffering—the "Cross of St. Michael"; promotes acceptance, calm, trust in life, and trust in the Goddess; heals fear at its source in this or past lifetimes.

Lepidolite with Mica • *(Causal Body Chakra)* • RED-VIOLET

Opens and develops the causal body chakra and spiritual body, stabilizes soul growth, balances psychic communication with earth-plane daily functioning, brings spiritual information into daily life, aids channeling and mediumship, promotes contact with spirit guides and angels.

See also Mica.

Lepidolite—Yellow • *(Solar Plexus)* • YELLOW

Calms fear, releases fears one at a time for viewing and letting go, opens and clears old outmoded fears, heals damage from psychic attacks, protects against psychic draining, dissolves cords and hooks but only from the solar plexus chakra, protects and shields the solar plexus chakra from incoming negative energy, acts as a chakra shield for the solar plexus.

Limonite • *(Solar Plexus)* • BROWN

Protects the solar plexus chakra from other people's jealousy, envy and negative thoughts; protects from psychic attacks;

works as a chakra shield for the solar plexus only; aids in the right use of will for oneself and recognition of wrong use in others; filters and balances energy.

Lodestone • *(Grounding)* • METALLIC BROWN

Protects the aura from negative energy and psychic attacks, clears negative energy from the aura by magnetism, balances aura energy and the acupuncture meridians; repels negativity back to its sender, creates a shield against harmful vibrations but lets positive energy through. *Note:* Lodestone is usually self-clearing and is used in pairs.

Magnetite • *(Grounding)* • METALLIC BROWN

Balances energy polarities and acupuncture meridians, opens blocked acupuncture points, aids the movement of Ch'i from the root chakra through the knees and feet; promotes grounding and ballast into the Earth, balances the Hara and Kundalini Line energy channels, helps one to be balanced through life and along one's chosen path.

Malachite • *(Solar Plexus)* • GREEN AND BLACK
Detoxifies the emotional body and brings the emotions into the physical body for release, releases negative and painful emotions, clears and releases old traumas from this life and past lives, brings things out from within; offers protection against psychic attack and other people's negativity, supports psychotherapy and emotional recovery processes, detoxifies the liver and gall bladder on the emotional level; traditionally used to aid childbirth labor and protects against poisoning. *Note:* Malachite's deep energy cleansing may not be comfortable; use it in small doses.

Malachite—Druzy • *(Solar Plexus)* • GREEN
Works on the kundalini level, cleanses and detoxifies the Kundalini Line of old traumas and negative emotions, brings things out from within, traditionally aids childbirth, provides psychic protection and filtering, supports those in therapy who are willing to do the emotional work intensively and quickly, releases the karma of old trauma by healing it emotionally, prevents this-life emotional negativity and trauma from becoming karmic. *Note:* The Druzy formation softens Malachite's effects and actions.

Malachite—Red • *(Belly)* • RED-ORANGE

Red Malachite is the commercial name for Red-Banded Jasper. It is not Malachite. *See* Jasper—Red-Banded.

Malachite Stalactites • *(Solar Plexus)* • GREEN

Use as for Druzy Malachite, but note that most of these gemstone specimens are reconstituted and man-made, rather than naturally found.

Marcasite • *(Vision)* • SILVER

Expands psychic vision, clairvoyance, and the ability to see discarnate entities and "ghosts"; protects and aids psychics who help discarnate entities pass over and de-haunt houses; aids in removal of spirit attachments, possessions, and entities in healing work and protects healers who do this work; provides protection from negative entities and energy.

Mariposite • *(Heart)* • GREEN AND WHITE

Reduces stress, calms and stabilizes, reduces fear, and reduces energy overload; lessens exhaustion; deepens and calms breathing; speeds regeneration and recovery; eases physical pain; use as an all-healing energy that functions like a mineral version of the flower essence Rescue Remedy.

Meteorite • *(Galactic Body Chakras)* • METALLIC

Provides a message from the stars that we on Earth are neither alone nor abandoned by the universe; promises that the quarantine of planet Earth will end and a time of hope and peace will come; brings aid from high-level Light Be-ings from other planets and dimensions; aids contact with other-planetary helpers and protection from negative alien energies.

Mica • *(Vision)* • SILVER

For perceiving the eyes as the windows of the soul, develops the vision chakras as reflectors of soul-level growth and development, aids understanding of the levels and layers of soul structure and the between-life state, enhances the psychic ability to visualize, promotes the ability to see the many layers of a situation from a spiritual perspective, helps in discerning reality and illusion.

See also Lepidolite with Mica.

Mica—Muscovite • *(Vision)* • SILVER

Sorts out one's thoughts, problems, and priorities and puts them in perspective; establishes a one-thing-at-a-time order; creates step-by-step processes for working out problems more easily; divides large problems and projects into smaller easy steps; aids concentration and focus; aids completing what one starts; reduces stress, promotes living in the present.

Microlite • *(Belly)* • ORANGE

Provides emotional support for women who wish to become pregnant and have difficulty conceiving; promotes conception, implanting of a fetus in a uterus, carrying gestation to term, and safe labor and delivery; provides emotional support for all the reasons why women who wish to have children can't have them; provides support during high-tech fertility treatments; helps women who don't conceive to accept childlessness or adoption.

Moldavite • *(Movement)* • DARK GREEN

Promotes connection with positive Pleiadian helpers and healers for protection, healing, and self-healing; aids removal of negative past-life and present-life alien implants; offers protection from negative alien interference; removes spirit attachments, entities, and spirit possessions; protects Earth healers and psychics who remove implants and attachments from others; promotes the freedom to move among the dimensions and planets while remaining safe on Earth; promotes other-planetary contact through dreams and meditation; protects astral travel; aids and enhances psychic opening.

Mookite • *See* Jasper—Mookite.

Moonstone—Blue • *(Throat)* • LIGHT BLUE
Focuses on the psychic abilities of empathy and telepathy, sending and receiving; promotes communicating psychically with people, pets, discarnate entities, plant or animal devas, Goddesses, spirit guides, and angels—Light Be-ings in or out of body; promotes communication with other-planetary Be-ings; aids psychic communication across time, dimension, space, and the galaxy; promotes honoring oneself as a psychic Be-ing and a part of the Goddess; aids self-blessing; aids psychic healing and psychic hearing (clairaudience).

Moonstone—Grey • *(Vision)* • SILVER-GREY

Focuses on the psychic abilities of vision and clairvoyance, psychic sight and knowing; creates new realities and understanding of realities other than those on the earth-plane; enhances visualization, meditation, guided journeys, shamanic journeys, and visual psychic healing; promotes seeing extra-terrestrials, discarnate entities, spirit guides, angels, Goddesses, devas, and Light Be-ings; expands one's spiritual and psychic vision, promotes seeing oneself as a part of the Goddess and the universal plan; aids in the ability to focus on one's life path.

Moonstone—Peach • *(Heart)* • PEACH AND PINK

Heals the heart by bringing the Goddess's love into it; promotes spiritual and psychic opening as heart and emotional healing; aids in discovering women's (and one's own) place in the universal plan; promotes discovering oneself as Goddess within; provides gentle clearing of heart scars and traumas from this life and past lives; aids in easing self-criticism and learning to be gentle with oneself; promotes acceptance and openness, learning to trust the Goddess and oneself, and honoring oneself as a woman; this is an all-healing energy specifically for women.

Moonstone—Rainbow • *(Transpersonal Point)* • WHITE

The stone is very fragile and susceptible to destruction by negative energies and entities. Protects against psychic attacks by drawing them to the stone—the stone often shatters or "dies" (becomes dark and lifeless) by doing so; repairs the transpersonal point and its connections and replaces those too damaged to repair; aids connection with the Light; supports channeling, healing, and all psychic work. *Note:* Rainbow Moonstone is not Moonstone, but White Labradorite. Colors in Rainbow Moonstone—Amethyst Rainbow Moonstone, Aqua Rainbow Moonstone, Purple Rainbow Moonstone, Red Onyx Rainbow Moonstone, Ruby Rainbow Moonstone, Sapphire Rainbow Moonstone—are dyed.

Moonstone—White • *(Third Eye)* • WHITE

Personifies women's connection to the Goddess and the moon; regulates menstrual and fertility cycles; eases menopause; promotes psychic "lunar" knowing, psychic sight, entrance into realities other than those on the earth-plane, intuition, ancient women's wisdom, magick and the Craft, and ritual; soothes and heals the emotions and mind; enhances spiritual growth and development; heals the astral body.

Moqui Marbles • *(Grounding)* • BROWN

For those who refuse to accept Earth and incarnation in the body; plants one firmly on the planet, binds one to earth-plane awareness and reality, focuses one's path on the earth plane, reduces psychic awareness, reduces escapism and daydreaming, grounds one firmly into body awareness, promotes discovery of the joys of being in a body, aids grounding after meditation and psychic work, grounds the kundalini. *Note:* Moqui Marbles are also called Shaman Stones.

Morganite (Pink Beryl) • *(Causal Body Chakra)* • PINK

Opens the causal body chakra so spiritual-level healing can be transmitted to the emotional body; raises the energy vibration of the emotional and astral levels; heals the astral body and the emotional heart; heals and returns fragmented soul parts; aids soul retrieval; aligns the astral and etheric bodies; heals karmic emotional pain, chronic karmic suffering, and past-life traumas.

Mother-of-Pearl—Black • *(Root)* • BLACK

Grounds, calms, soothes, stabilizes, and comforts grief and depression; accesses the positive darkness where germination and new growth happen; promotes healing dreams and protects during sleep and in the dream state; promotes knowing that everything is all right; promotes patient waiting when waiting is needed; provides certainty that the Light is always there—even in the dark.

Mother-of-Pearl—Blister Pearl

(Transpersonal Point) • OFF-WHITE

Calms in urgent situations and life crises; comforts, soothes, and reduces stress and fear; promotes knowing that "this too will pass" and all will come right; soothes people who are dying or facing a life-challenging sickness or surgery. *Note:* Blister Pearl is an unfinished formation of Pearl inside the pearl oyster shell.

Mother-of-Pearl—Natural

(Transpersonal Point) • OFF-WHITE, TAN

Calms and soothes physically and emotionally, insulates against irritants, eases discomfort in crowds or around other people; reduces desire to hide in the background, creating a sense of safety and desire to participate; aids in receiving the comfort of the Light.

Mother-of-Pearl—White • *(Third Eye)* • WHITE
Soothes, reduces stress and worry, aids knowing that everything is okay, promotes seeing a positive reality, helps to heal the friction in one's life, aids learning to flow with life, provides a sense of safety and security, provides emotional shelter, brings in the all-nurturing Mother Goddess, balances physical energy, supports the lymphatic and immune systems.

Mugglestone (Hematite and Jasper)
(Grounding) • BLACK AND TAN
Focuses one's energy on the body and the earth-plane; grounds, centers, and balances; protects the integrity of the etheric double aura from tears and rips; repairs the damaged aura envelope; protects against and repels psychic attacks; gathers and calms scattered energies; reduces stress particularly when induced by conflicts with other people; aids recovery from anesthetics and surgeries; reduces bleeding traditionally.

Natrolite • *(Transpersonal Point)* • CLEAR, WHITE
Promotes Hara Line alignment and opening; aids focusing and setting and meeting goals; helps adapt to circumstances;

stimulates psychic opening; raises vibration levels to bring in the Light; promotes channeling and ascension; raises the vibrations and effects of other gemstones when used with them; aids shape shifters; supports bones and the brain. *Note:* Natrolite turns bright green under fluorescent lighting.

Neptunite • *(Earth)* • BLACK

Offers connection with the waters and water Be-ings of the Earth and stars; promotes communication with dolphins, whales, fish, sea creatures, other-planetary cetaceans, water devas, mermaids, and water Goddesses; promotes connection with the Well of Life at the Earth's core; balances the water element in the body; reduces water retention in the body; supports circulatory healing; cleanses the blood.

Nuumite • *(Vision)* • BLACK

Opens the vision chakras; promotes having visions and understanding them; promotes receiving visual psychic information; aids in using the eyes to transmit psychic energy for distance healing; aids using the eyes as lasers for psychic surgery; promotes insight and intuition; clears and heals the auric field of tears, holes, rips and blockages; regenerates the aura; helps to regenerate the eyes. *Note:* Nuumite is a powerful new gemstone from Greenland; watch for faceted Nuumite in jewelry.

Obsidian—Aqua • *(Thymus)* • AQUA

Connects the heart, throat, and thymus chakras; interfaces the Hara and Kundalini Lines; promotes deep peace; heals emotional pain and grief, invokes the free flowing of the water element in the physical body; aids psychic telepathy and empathy; enhances reception of psychic information; enhances animal communication, communication with devas and nature spirits, and communication with water devas; aids psychic healing; supports the heart, lungs, throat, immune system, vision, and hearing; encourages creativity of all kinds; energizes and opens. *Note:* This lovely natural volcanic glass is commercially called Aqua Lemuria.

Obsidian—Black • *(Earth)* • BLACK

Promotes grounding into the Earth's origins and the soul's origins on other planets, opens awareness of past lives, reveals awareness of negative karma to clear and heal it, promotes body awareness and centers the soul into this incarnation, grounds the Spirit into the physical body after psychic work, stabilizes and reduces fear and panic states, promotes grounding and centering, supports scrying and past-life regression. *Note:* Obsidian is a natural volcanic glass.

Obsidian—Blue • *(Throat)* • BLUE
Connects the energies of the throat, and thymus chakras, in the Kundalini and Hara Lines; creates a sense of floating or flying—the elements of air; aids one's ability to flow, or float, with change; heals the fear of change; heals fears and phobias; eases resistance; provides balance and confidence; aids the ability to verbalize one's thoughts, fears and needs so they can be resolved; promotes a sense of peace and the knowledge that everything will be all right. *Note:* Another name for this natural volcanic glass is Tengizite.

Obsidian—Cobalt Blue • *(Third Eye)* • INDIGO
Accesses the element of Spirit; represents he element of air, creates a sense of floating or flying; provides a sense of being lifted up and held in strong arms, protected, kept safe;

dissolves fear; promotes confidence and self-confidence; promotes the ability to accept change and see its spiritual meaning; protects from and dissolves negative energies; dissolves illusions; promotes the ability to see spiritual truth in any situation. *Note:* Also called Tengizite, this stone is a form of natural volcanic glass.

Obsidian—Green • *(Heart)* • GREEN

Provides a sense of free-flowing movement that moves from the heart to the feet and settles in the root chakra; accesses the essence of the water element; promotes relaxation, calm, peace, and a sigh of relief; reduces stress; eases insomnia; protects against nightmares; promotes the ability to flow with change, aids the ability to accept and recognize that change is inevitable; promotes confidence in outcomes and the knowledge that everything will be all right. *Note:* A form of natural volcanic glass, Green Obsidian is also called Gaia Stone.

Obsidian—Mahogany • *(Earth)* • BROWN AND BLACK

Grounds and roots one's life purpose into healing the planet; promotes Earth stewardship, activism, and environmentalism;

aids psychic healers who focus on Earth healing and activists who work against species extinction; aids animals, reptiles, birds, insects, and plants or the land and seas; supports and prevents burnout and discouragement; aids communication with nonhuman species and nature devas. *Note:* Obsidian is a natural volcanic glass.

Obsidian—Purple Sheen • *(Earth)* • BLACK
Promotes connection with the Lords of Karma, heals one's past lives and current karma in this lifetime, heals the past to heal the present and future, aids rewriting one's Akashic Record, aids past-life regression and future-life progression; aids in understanding one's present lifetime in terms of what has gone before and healing the difficulties permanently, heals karmic patterns and negative karma. *Note:* Obsidian is a natural volcanic glass.

Obsidian—Rainbow • *(Earth)* • BLACK
Brings soul awareness into the body, spiritualizes this incarnation for greater soul growth, aids karmic healing, understanding of how past lives have created present life

situations, aids healing karmic patterns and releasing the damage of the past, promotes working with the Lords of Karma and Divine Director for enlightenment in this lifetime, aids in becoming an old soul. *Note:* Obsidian is a natural volcanic glass.

Obsidian—Red • *(Perineum)* • RED

Connects the Kundalini Line root chakra with the Hara Line perineum chakra, connects the Hara and Kundalini Lines; accesses the element of fire through the microcosmic orbit—a hot, yang gemstone; provides hot warming energy; energizes; grounds and opens the root chakra; promotes determination, focus, self-confidence, and the ability to ignore one's fears and move beyond them; supports those who practice Tai Ch'i—it moves the energy. *Note:* Red Obsidian is a natural volcanic glass.

Obsidian—Snowflake • *(Earth)* • BLACK AND WHITE

Opens the awareness of past lives and of having had many incarnations; promotes the knowledge that we have been here before and will be here again, that there is no death of the soul; aids in past life meditation and regression work, understanding the present in terms of the past, and healing karma and karmic patterns.

Obsidian—Vitrophyre • *(Hara Chakra)* • BROWN AND GOLD
Develops, repairs, and connects the hara chakra and entire Hara Line; good for those who wander aimlessly through life with no sense of purpose; establishes one's life purpose and puts one on the path; contains bursting flowers of Light; heals the karma of rootlessness. *Note:* Vitrophyre is a rare brown form of obsidian with gold flower-like inclusions.

Okenite • *(Galactic Body Chakras)* • WHITE
Opens and clears the Light Body for connection to the mind grid, Earth grid, and creation grid; makes one a channel for other-planetary aid to Earth; extends one's perceptions beyond Earth and into the stars; opens and clears Earthly limitations of being bound to the planet or the body; transforms limitations and karma; good for star people serving on Earth. *Note*: This stone is not of Earth origin.

Onyx—Black • *(Earth)* • BLACK

Heals grief that has gone on too long; promotes knowing that there is no death; aids in understanding the Wheel of birth, death, and rebirth; fosters knowing that separation is an illusion and reunion will come; promotes psychic contact with those who have died through séances, mediumship, and messages from the dead; aids past-life and between-lives regression work; supports future-life progressions; prevents and removes spirit possessions; promotes the feeling of being hidden from evil and protected by the Light; promotes feeling watched over by angels, feeling loved; eases loneliness; supports going on alone.

Onyx—Blue • *(Third Eye)* • BLUE

Carries the energy of Isis; opens, heals, clears, and activates the third eye chakra, mental body, mind grid, and Ka template; aids in bringing in one's Higher Self; heals soul fragments and helps with soul retrieval; promotes ascension; removes obstructions to mental body healing; promotes contact with spirit guides, angels, and Goddess; aids psychic communication with animals and contact with dolphins and whales; quiets the mind.

Onyx—Green • *(Movement)* • DARK GREEN
Heals karma that is obstructing progress on one's life path, clears the path to growth and movement, promotes achievement; manifests one's spiritual growth on the earth-plane, heals confusion or resistance to one's life agreements; promotes forward progress, provides emotional support for painful knees.

Onyx—Mexican White • *(Movement)* • WHITE, TAN, GREEN
Stabilizes, promotes steadfastness, aids being immovable where refusal to move or change is positive, breaks a pattern of immovability when change is needed and required. *Note:* Mexican Onyx is not a strong healing energy but is useful for a few people, mostly men.

Onyx—Pḥa Sapha (Black Hills)
(Diaphragm) • BEIGE AND WHITE
Aligns the Hara Line channels and chakras; promotes a dual flow of Ch'i from the head to the feet and from the feet to the head; promotes steady energy flow for cleansing and purification; removes blockages; supports Tai Ch'i and yoga practitioners; aids the microcosmic orbit; promotes

stability, prosperity, good luck, and protection; aids self-confidence and self-control.

Opal—Blue • *(Throat)* • BLUE, GREY, AND WHITE
Intensifies the need and ability to express emotions and creativity; aids the expression of repressed emotions; opens communication between people; opens communication between people and pets, people and spirit guides, and people and Light Be-ings; aids psychic hearing, sending and receiving, encouraging empathy and telepathy; soothes the throat; opens the voice; calms.

Opal—Boulder • *(Hara Chakra)* • IRIDESCENT BROWN
Collects and condenses energy in the hara chakra; aids knowing and manifesting one's life purpose; awakens spirituality, aids finding one's path and one's reason for living in this incarnation; releases strong bursts of propulsive energy through the Hara Line; emits bursts of Light to cleanse, heal, repair, open, and awaken; aids spiritual evolution and ascension; gets one moving. *Note:* Opals amplify energy.

Opal—Mexican Fire • *(Belly)* • ORANGE AND WHITE

Lights the fires of positive sexuality and sexual healing; opens the pictures held in the belly chakra; releases and heals memories of incest, rape, and sexual abuse; aids in leaving battered or abusive relationships; helps to establish new relationships after trauma; supports healthy sexuality and healthy sexual relationships—gay or heterosexual, promotes the ability to orgasm.

Opal—Oregon • *(Transpersonal Point)* • WHITE

Heals and releases past emotional traumas from this life and past lives; cleanses and heals the emotional body and etheric double aura envelope; promotes positive nurturing and self-nurturing; releases and relieves; returns and heals lost soul fragments in the soul retrieval process; protects soul fragments during healing; supports imagination, childlike vulnerability, joyful rediscovery of self, positivity, and peace.

Opal—Owhyee Blue • *(Throat)* • BLUE

Heals the throat on all levels; promotes reception of psychic information; encourages creativity, speech, and speaking out;

supports telepathy and empathy, especially with animals; amplifies reception and receptivity; helps to express feelings and speak one's truth; aids psychic hearing; clears throat issues from this life and past lives; aids in understanding karmic patterns so they can be released; purifies and cleanses; provides contact with the angelic realm. *Note:* Owhyee Blue Opal has a cerulean-blue gemstone with a feminine energy of great purity.

Opal—White • *(Crown)* • WHITE
Opens and amplifies the energy of all the kundalini chakras, fills the Kundalini Line with color and Light; amplifies negative patterns and behaviors for the purpose of clearing and releasing them; raises the kundalini, and increases Light and spiritual awareness, promotes spiritual initiation. *Note:* Use White Opal with Rose Quartz for positivity and balance.

Opal Aura Crystal • *(Transpersonal Point)* • IRIDESCENT WHITE
Promotes harmony and peace within and without; aligns the energy bodies; brings clarity of emotions and mind; soothes, comforts, and heals the transpersonal point chakra and entire Hara Line; aids connection with the angelic realm and nature

devas. *Note:* This stone is also known as Angel Aura or Pearl Aura Crystal and is made by irradiating and bonding Zircon to Clear Quartz.

See also Aqua Aura Crystal, Cobalt Aura Crystal, Opal Aura Crystal, Rainbow Aura Crystal, Rose Aura Crystal, and Silver Aura Crystal.

Orpiment—Orange • *(Hara Chakra)* • ORANGE
Helps to manifest one's life purpose and path; transforms ideas into actions; promotes actively doing the work of one's life purpose; connects intellect to action, aids studying and learning, conceptualization, organization, and memory; takes quantities of isolated facts and forms them into a unified whole, aids in finding the relationships among ideas; promotes the ability to compare and contrast ideas.

Orpiment—Yellow • *(Solar Plexus)* • YELLOW
Balances psychic energy and impressions that enter through the solar plexus chakra, clears the solar plexus chakra and mental body; aids right use of will and protection from other

people's attempts at manipulation; protects from other people's negativity, stimulates energy; aids intellectual and mental clarity, aids studying and learning.

Paint Stone • *(Perineum)* • RED AND TAN
Grounds; connects to the Earth's core; connects with Earth Goddesses like Gaia, Demeter, or the Old One; aids girls at menarche (their first period), helping them adjust to being a woman; honors femininity, creation, fertility, woman as a life-giver, pride in being female, and growing from child to woman. *Note:* Paint Stone is also called Indian Paint Stone; it is a variety of Rhyolite.

Peacock Ore • *(Third Eye)* • METALLIC COLORS
Opens the third eye, or brow chakra; stimulates psychic opening, psychic vision and clairvoyance, and inner knowing; promotes self-confidence on one's path; provides certainty of what one sees psychically; helps psychics learning to trust their abilities; enhances distance healing; helps to create one's own reality manifest it by visualization. *Note:* Peacock Ore is also called Peacock Rock or Bornite.

Pearl • *(Crown)* • WHITE

Soothes and heals the negativity and struggle in one's life, surrounds negative energy with Light, dissolves negative energy, heals negative thoughts and thought forms, moves attachments and psychic attacks out of the aura, releases negative karmic patterns, fills the aura with healing Light, calms and soothes the emotions, heals the negative inner voice and sub-personalities.

Pecos Diamond • *(Belly)* • ORANGE

Transforms and transmutes anger; changes anger and rage from this life and past lives to understanding, forgiveness and self-forgiveness; helps heal past sexual abuse, emotional abuse, rape, and battering; releases karmic patterns of abuse from the aura; heals the inner child, helps to release chakra cords from all the kundalini chakras; protects clairsentient healers who take on other people's symptoms; releases matching pictures between a healer and the healing recipient; expands compassion for others and oneself. *Note:* Pecos Diamond is also called Pecos Quartz.

Pectolite • *See* Larimar.

Peridot • *(Diaphragm)* • YELLOW-GREEN
Balances the process of emotional release and healing; regulates detoxification of emotions to comfortable levels; heals emotional and physical pain; lightens suffering; promotes emotional balance, fosters security and inner peace; promotes and enhances abundance and prosperity; supports physical detoxification and the assimilation organs—liver, kidneys, bladder, gall bladder, and stomach; helps to heal ulcers, irritable bowel syndrome, and kidney infections. *Note:* An older name for Peridot is Olivine, not to be confused with Olivine Jade, which is a form of Serpentine.

Peruvian Opal • *See* Andean Opal.

Petalite—Clear • *(Transpersonal Point)* • CLEAR
Furthers one's connection and communication with the Light; contacts and interacts with angels, devas, the Lords of Karma, Goddesses, spirit guides, animals, and Light Be-ings; promotes psychic development and opening, psychic communication, and ability to channel and do automatic writing; aids access to the Akashic Records and the collective mind grid; promotes communication with the dead; aids séance mediumship.

Petalite—Pink • *(Heart)* • PINK
Brings Light into the heart; promotes connection with Light Be-ings of all kinds for healing, comfort, and unconditional love; enhances communication with spirit guides, angels, Goddesses, and discarnate healers and helpers; heals the heart and emotional body; opens the heart to love; calms and stabilizes; changes grief and hurt to joy; promotes knowing one is loved and not alone. *Note:* This rare stone resembles Rose Quartz physically and energetically; of the two, Petalite is the stronger energy.

Petoskey Stone • *(Third Eye)* • GREY
Balances and reduces third-eye visions and impressions, reduces psychic visions, brings one back to Earth after channeling, grounds and balances, helps people who can't turn off their psychic senses at will, supports people who are overloaded and overwhelmed with psychic visions of disasters and wish to stop or control them, supports people who have trouble grounding after psychic work.

Petrified Wood • *(Movement)* • TAN AND GREEN

For those unable to persevere on their life path and life goal; aids concentration, grounding, and centering; heals being scattered, flighty, or indecisive; helps those who cannot complete what they start; promotes setting and keeping goals; encourages steadiness and stability; aids slowing down; helps the spirit to function in the body.

Phenacite—White • *(Transpersonal Point)* • WHITE, CLEAR

Activates the Hara Line chakras and the emotional body; brings Heavenly Ch'i/Goddess energy into the Hara Line and Kundalini chakras, channels, and meridians; fills the aura's electrical system with Light and information; increases Light flow through the aura, chakras and channels; aligns the aura bodies; balances, comforts and stabilizes; promotes core soul healing; develops full-complement DNA; heals traumas and damage to the aura field on all body levels; offers energy protection; provides awareness of one's self as part of a greater Goddess plan. *Note:* This is a very intense energy that is best taken in small doses; it is not for wearing all the time or for use by most people.

Phenacite—Yellow • *(Transpersonal Point)* • GOLDEN

Clears, purifies and opens the transpersonal point chakra and the entire Hara Line; aids development of the Hara Line chakras and channels; aligns and harmonizes; brings in the Light; promotes spiritual transformation; puts one on the ascension path. *Note:* This strong, transformative energy may be too intense, take in small doses.

Picasso Stone • *(Earth)* • BLACK AND BROWN

Opens the galactic chakras to achieve contact with positive other-planetary Be-ings while remaining grounded on Earth; aids contact with other-planetary Earth guardians and Earth healers; acts as a spaceship receiver; shields against negative aliens and entities; aids star people incarnated in Earth bodies; aids psychics who do Earth healing; promotes channeling, intuition, creativity, inspiration, and knowledge of the stars.

Picture Sandstone • *(Diaphragm)* • TAN

Aids scrying, contains a record of the Earth's formation; meditate with it to promote visions of the newborn Earth; contains visions of Earth's past, present, and future; promotes visions of one's own past, present, and future; keeps a record of time in a planetary and a personal timeline.

Pietersite—Black • *(Earth)* • BLACK

Aids one's connection to the planet, promotes grounding and protection; filters Earth toxins and energies so they don't enter the body, cleanses Earth toxins from the body, protects from the negative mass consciousness, brings the spirit into the body, cleanses both spirit and body, repairs spirit connection with the body and the Earth, repels negative forces and entities. *Note:* Pietersite is also called Tempest Stone.

Pietersite—Blue • *(Third Eye)* • INDIGO AND BLACK

Aids psychic opening, channeling, and receiving psychic information; clears, repairs and opens the third eye chakra; protects the third eye chakra; repels negative forces and entities; aids connection with the Light; heals the Spirit, which connects the Light with physical form; removes blockages from the third eye and crown chakras. *Note:* Pietersite is also called Tempest Stone.

Pietersite—Brown • *(Grounding)* • BROWN AND BLACK
Promotes grounding, connection to the planet and the Light, and stability; protects from negative forces and entities; protects from the negative mass consciousness; repairs the grounding system and all of its connections, chakras, templates, and components; heals the soul-body connective structure; makes the positive mass consciousness available to the individual mind. *Note:* Pietersite is also called Tempest Stone.

Pietersite—Gold • *(Hara Chakra)* • GOLD AND RED
Cleanses, heals, and protects the hara chakra; protects one's life purpose and the ability to manifest it; repairs and reconnects; brings the Light in to aid one's life purpose on a daily basis; brings in nourishment from the Earth's core and the Well of Life; guides one's choosing, attaining, and implementing one's karmic purpose for this incarnation. *Note:* Pietersite is also called Tempest Stone.

Pietersite—Red • *(Perineum)* • RED
Cleanses, repairs, connects, heals, and protects the perineum chakra; protects one's life force and this incarnation; provides

the vitality to achieve one's life purpose and maintain one's life in body; offers connection to the Earth and the Earth core; brings in nourishment from the Well of Life and the Earth core; brings in the Light to protect one's life; promotes grounding, the will to live, the will to achieve, and the will to manifest one's life purpose. *Note:* Pietersite is also called Tempest Stone.

Pipestone • *(Root)* • RED

Represents the blood of the ancestors of Native Minnesotans, Native American heritage, the suffering of the people, and the survival of the people and traditions; represents the Great Mystery of all life (Buddhist Void, Wiccan Goddess), life itself, and the sacredness and oneness of all life. Note: Pipestone is sacred to Native people and is not for mundane or profane use. It is made into bowls for sacred ritual smoking pipes.

Prasiolite • *(Heart)* • GREEN

Prasiolite is color-treated Quartz and is also called Green Amethyst; it does not occur naturally. Its properties are similar to Natural Citrine. *See* Citrine—Natural.

Prehnite • *(Heart)* • GREEN

Soothes, aids heart healing and grief healing; reduces stress; provides a sense of calm and wellness, relief, the feeling that everything will be all right; accesses the element of water; connects with water devas and mermaids; provides the feeling of free flowing in one's life; connects with the angelic realm; provides emotional support for heart dis-ease and high blood pressure.

Psilomelane • *(Earth)* • BLACK

Promotes working to access and clear karma; aids in contacting and working with the Lords of Karma and Divine Director; aids in obtaining karmic information, karmic release, and dispensation; helps to heal karmic patterns; clears one's karma from all lifetimes and all planets; promotes work leading to ascension at advanced levels; clears the Hara Line of negativity and obstructions; promotes grounding into the Earth, the physical body, this incarnation. *Note:* Psilomelane is also called Crown of Silver or Black Malachite for its silver patterns on shiny black. It is not malachite.

Pumice • *(Heart)* • PINK

Eases abrasiveness that creates difficulty in one's life; helps to open the heart and get beyond old pain and defenses; promotes gentleness and vulnerability, supports the ability to give to others and to let others be close; aids emotional healing, recovery, and the ability to trust; helps old emotional wounds heal by letting the Light in. *Note:* This is not a major healing energy but useful for some people.

Purpurite • *(Causal Body Chakra)* • RED-VIOLET

For spiritual manifesting (commercial and noncommercial), aids manifesting one's highest good materially and nonmaterially; promotes manifesting one's life path, fulfilling karmic agreements. and following one's life purpose; clears, opens, and activates the causal body chakra; aids opening to channel and to receiving positive discarnate help; promotes communication with spirit guides and angels; receives psychic information and knowing.

Pyrite • *(Solar Plexus)* • METALLIC GOLD

Promotes higher-level energy assimilation and manifesting,

promotes the stability of energy levels and what comes in through the energy channels, aids in receiving expanded amounts of energy and Light without becoming scattered or stressed, promotes optimal use of psychic energy, calms, aids prosperity and the ability to manifest earth-plane needs and abundance, uplifts and grounds simultaneously.

Pyrite with Magnetite • *See* Apache Gold.

Pyromorphite • *(Earth)* • BLACK AND MULTICOLORED
Fosters a soul connection to all Earth's life forms; promotes compassion for all Be-ings on the planet; aids psychic communication with plant and mineral devas, nature spirits, insects, trees, and animals; promotes the awareness that all life is one life and that what harms one harms all; for stewardship of the Earth, Earth healing.

Quartz—Black • *(Earth)* • BLACK
Promotes psychic protection; prevents negative energies from entering the aura or chakras; protects from both deliberate and random negativity and evil; protects from the negative mass

consciousness; filters out the pain of individuals and groups, especially in the case of Earth change disasters; grounds and insulates. *Note:* Black Quartz differs from Smoky Quartz in that it is not translucent but a solid matte finish black. Use it in natural form only, not the irradiated clear Quartz Crystal that is burnt black and has no healing ability.

Quartz—Blue • *(Third Eye)* • BLUE

Opens and stimulates the third eye chakra to enhance psychic ability and spirituality; promotes telepathy, clairvoyance, psychic healing, contact with guides and angels, and psychic vision; promotes seeing the world in a spiritual rather than an earth-plane way; switches earth-plane illusion to spiritual reality; stabilizes new psychics. *Note:* Blue Quartz is also called Siderite.

Quartz—Cactus • *See* Quartz—Spirit.

Quartz—Candle • *(Movement)* • TAN AND CLEAR

Protects people whose forward movement in life is hesitant or difficult; aids and supports changes of direction that lead to manifesting one's life purpose; promotes changing one's life to accomplish one's goals; supports positive emotional and lifestyle changes; eases inflexibility, stubbornness, and procrastination; transforms negativity; integrates the physical with the spiritual; offers support for the bones, hips, legs, and knees.

Quartz—Cherry • *(None)* • CLEAR AND RED
Cherry Quartz is synthetic, made by melting raw crystal and adding copper powder for the red internal streaks. There are no healing uses; buyers beware.

Quartz—Chlorite Inclusion • *(Diaphragm)* • GREEN AND CLEAR
Detoxifies the Kundalini and Hara Lines; supports the removal of chemical toxins, petroleum and pesticides from body tissues and all aura levels; clears environmental pollutants from the aura and physical body; processes air and water pollution; supports people with environmental illness, chronic fatigue, cancer, asthma, and liver damage.

Quartz—Cinnabar • *(Entire Hara Line)* • BLACK, WHITE, RED
Connects and activates the Hara Line grounding system; opens

the perineum chakra, grounding chakras, and Earth chakras; connects the Hara Line to the Earth's core; aids grounding and stability; promotes manifesting the divine pattern and plan for this lifetime on Earth; aids manifesting one's karmic plan and agreements; sustains and supports this incarnation; balances the life force. *Note:* This stone combines Cinnebar, Dolomite, and Quartz.

Quartz—Clear Crystal • *(Transpersonal Point)* • CLEAR

Fills the aura, chakras, templates and bodies with Light; heals and aligns the etheric and emotional bodies; clears negativity at all levels; protects from negative energy; detoxifies the aura; promotes and intensifies spiritual expansion and awareness, aids enlightenment; aids emotional stability; supports all physical and emotional dis-eases; speeds healing; brings Light and goodness on every level; promotes connection and communication with the Light and Light Be-ings.

Quartz—Crystal Ball • *(Transpersonal Point)* • CLEAR

Basic tool for scrying and obtaining psychic information in the form of visual images; promotes communication with the

Light, aids reception of psychically-derived information and channeling; aids in seeing the past, present, or future; aids in seeing or locating people, animals or objects; enhances visualization and meditation; obtains visual imagery and information of all kinds. *Note:* Crystal Balls for scrying can be made of many kinds of gemstones and they can be of any size. This information is primarily for Clear Quartz Crystal Balls.

Quartz—Crystal Skull • *(Transpersonal Point)* • CLEAR
Receives energy; regenerates the mental body and mind grid; repairs, reprograms, cleanses, and purifies; helps to establish and reestablish connection with the Light; connects with the positive collective consciousness and Earth grid consciousness; brings in information from the Light; enhances communication with Light Be-ings; supports channeling, healing, automatic writing, meditation, and studying; enhances psychic communication of all types. *Note:* The crystal skull form of quartz can be carved from any gemstone or from clear Quartz Crystal; it is a very ancient use of gemstone energy. Each type of stone adds its properties to the skull's form. The definition here is for the skull carving itself.

Quartz—Druzy • *(Third Eye)* • WHITE

Soothes and comforts, promotes stability and calms, opens the psychic abilities but stabilizes the user so information comes through in a balanced way, slows down information so it can be easily grasped, slows down streaming visions and images for easier comprehension; filters out negative energies, promotes connections with Light Be-ings that would otherwise be too powerful to hold.

Quartz—Elestial or Skeletal • *(Grounding)* • GREY-BROWN

Transforms, transitions, and changes; promotes soul growth; grounds one in one's life path; sets one on one's path, shows "where you are going" and how to begin getting there; can cause sudden and drastic aura and life path shifts at times; activates karmic correction after straying off one's path; promotes fulfillment of karmic agreements and one's life purpose; initiates deep releasing.

Quartz—Faden

(Transpersonal Point) • CLEAR, WHITE, PINK INCLUSIONS

Aids and supports the search for and attraction of one's true mate; promotes the energy attraction and the binding/joining/merging of energy between mates; makes one aware of past lives together and aids in healing damage from past lives to the present relationship; strengthens astral lovers' relationships and astral love-making; heals the ripping apart of Twin Flames in this and other incarnations; joins lovers at the Hara Line and hara chakras; heals and reunites damaged twin souls.

Quartz—Fairy • *See* Spirit Quartz.

Quartz—Fire (Lepidochrosite Inclusion) • *(Heart)* • DEEP PINK
Opens the heart chakra and the emotional body for major transformations and healing, opens the closed heart, prepares for deep psychic healing and karmic change, exposes and heals blocked past traumas from past lives and this life, removes past life barriers to heart healing in this lifetime, supports incest survivors and survivors of rape and battering, helps to ease post-traumatic stress, aids in becoming whole hearted.

Quartz—Flower of Life • *(Transpersonal Point)* • CLEAR
Manifests "as above so below"; brings the purity and power of

the Light above into the physical be-ing and body below; raises physical (body) vibrations up to meet the Light; promotes cleansing, purity, ascension, aura repair and healing, and all-healing; aids channeling. *Note:* Flower of Life is a clear Quartz Crystal that is precision cut into a multifaceted six-sided Star of David form. Other gemstones besides clear Quartz can be cut this way, as well.

Quartz—Fluorite Inclusion • *(Crown)* • CLEAR WITH INCLUSION
Stimulates the mind and brain; aids in reprogramming the mind to heal traits one wishes to change; helps one stop smoking; helps to improve study habits; promotes all positive habits; changes negative habits for positive ones; promotes better memory, better efficiency, and better use of mind and brain power of all kinds; increases mental ability of all kinds; promotes better use of time and energy. *Note:* Fluorite Included Quartz is a new find from Madagascar and is still very expensive.

Quartz—Girasol • *(Crown)* • OPALIZED
Aids visualization, psychic vision, seeing the past or future,

and seeing into simultaneous realities; promotes altered states and trance channeling; obtains psychic information; good teaching crystal, helps healers to see root sources of dis-ease and release them; this is an excellent scrying stone or crystal ball, very visual in all its uses. *Note:* Girasol Quartz is from Brazil; do not confuse it with Oregon Opal or Opal Quartz.

Quartz—Green (Prase) • *(Heart)* • LIGHT GREEN
Soothes, calms, and refills the heart after emotional release; repairs the heart chakra after opening a heart scar; provides Kwan Yin energy of compassion and universal love; promotes love for oneself and others; heals abandonment, loneliness, and emotional upset; aids heart and emotional body healing; eases fear and panic attacks.

Quartz—Grey Phantom • *(Vision)* • GREY AND CLEAR
Releases past-life information in visual flashbacks that move rapidly backward from recent to older scenes in this life, and then back into past lives; use briefly then stop to process the information; ask to focus on a specific lifetime or karmic

problem to be released; valuable for past life regression and for work on releasing karmic issues and patterns; use the information to work with the Lords of Karma; very valuable tool for karmic healing.

Quartz—Lordite Inclusion

(Causal Body Chakra) • RED, GREY, AND BROWN

Clears interference to psychic transmission; aids channeling, psychic healing, and reception of psychic information; helps with the "gutted fish" feeling after receiving major energy work; balances energy shifts in the aura; brings energy changes from the aura into the physical level; strengthens contact and communication with Light Be-ings, the Goddess, spirit guides, angels, the Lords of Karma, and ascended healers and teachers; calms and stabilizes.

Quartz—Moroccan Druzy • *(Perineum)* • ROSE-RED

Pulls energy downward through the Hara Line and into the perineum chakra and root chakra; connects the perineum chakra with the root chakra; connects the Hara and Kundalini Lines, grounds the Kundalini; stimulates sexuality; the life force and energy stimulant; eases exhaustion, low vitality, chronic fatigue, and burnout.

Quartz—Pecos • *See* Pecos Diamond.

Quartz—Purple Druzy • *(Crown)* • PURPLE
Amplifies spiritual opening; promotes opening to Goddess; clears the entire Kundalini Line and kundalini chakras; detoxifies, cleanses, and purifies; removes obstructions and blockages; clears negativity; serves as an astringent; supports healing the spine and central nervous system, vision, brain, and lymphatic system; stabilizes mental and nervous systems; calms.

Quartz—Red • *(Hara Chakra)* • RED-BROWN
Calms and grounds kundalini energy into the hara chakra, connects the Kundalini and Hara channels, aids in opening the Hara Line chakras and balancing the kundalini chakras, balances and focuses earth-plane and spiritual energy, promotes living as a spiritual Be-ing while incarnated in a body, provides support for blood circulation dis-eases and red blood cells.

Quartz—Red Hair • *(Root)* • CLEAR OR RED

Activates the root chakra; promotes love of life, zest for life, joy with each day's living, and gratitude; makes one aware of the connection between Above and Below; promotes connection with the Light and bringing the Light into physical form; fosters one's connection with the Earth and one's life force; encourages joy, laughter, love, sexuality, and fertility. *Note:* Red Hair Quartz is Rutilated Quartz Crystal with reddish inclusions, instead of the usual gold or silver.

Quartz—Red Phantom • *(Belly)* • ORANGE AND CLEAR

Opens and releases memories, feelings and pictures of past traumas and emotional pain in this life; heals and releases anger, rage, resentment, terror, fear, and confusion; aids the recovery process for sexual-abuse survivors and those who were abandoned or abused as children; heals a hurt inner child by awakening one's ability to feel and process what had to be blocked to survive; heals the emotional body. *Note:* Use Red Phantom Quartz in small doses.

Quartz—Rose • *(Heart)* • PINK
Promotes heart healing by encouraging positive self-love, self-esteem, self-image, and body image; aids opening to the Goddess and the Goddess within; heals the emotional body, aids learning to feel one's emotions; eases heartache, loneliness, emotional release and clearing; promotes acceptance, inner peace, forgiveness and self-forgiveness; eases fear; soothes grief; comforts. *Note:* Gem quality or crystalline Rose Quartz is the strongest and clearest energy. Rose Quartz and Amethyst are probably the most known and most used healing gemstones.

Quartz—Rutilated • *(Transpersonal Point)* • CLEAR OR GOLD
Expands the transmission of Light and psychic information entering the aura bodies, clears and expands the Hara Line and Kundalini channels and chakras, magnifies all positive energy entering the aura system, dispels all negative energy and energy blockages, speeds opening and releasing, intensifies all healing, balances the brain's hemispheres.

Quartz—Scepter • *(Crown)* • WHITE

Opens the crown to receive the Light; facilitates psychic guidance, communication, and channeling; promotes receiving psychic information; clears, repairs, and opens the templates that connect the energy bodies; promotes ascension; aids psychic healing and all psychic work; energizes and uplifts.

Quartz—Seer Stone • *(Transpersonal Point)* • CLEAR, WHITE

Record keeper of time and time lines; aids and amplifies visualization, clairvoyance, psychic seeing, and reading; gives visions of this life and past lives; aids far-seeing, seeing the distance or future for oneself or in readings for others; promotes ascension for more advanced psychics; calms; aids dream work, fills the aura with Light at the Hara Line and kundalini levels. *Note:* Seer Stone is a river-tumbled natural crystal ball or scrying stone, polished on one side for clarity.

Quartz—Smoky • *(Grounding)* • BROWN

Aids grounding into this incarnation, accepting the body and the earth-plane; promotes stability, security, and safety; encourages walking softly on the Earth Mother; promotes

Earth awareness and responsibility, accepting one's place on the planet; heals fear, depression, addictions, obsessions, spaciness, and ungroundedness.

Quartz—Smoky (Rutilated) • *(Grounding)* • METALLIC BROWN
Aids grounding into one's body and the present incarnation; grounds planetary consciousness in one's awareness and body; aids in accepting one's place on the planet and feeling a oneness with the Earth; promotes Earth stewardship, walking softly on the Earth Mother and developing Earth awareness and responsibility; promotes manifesting one's life purpose; helps to heal the body of all dis-ease; creates security and safety; heals fear, depression, addictions, and obsessions; stabilizes neurological systems.

Quartz—Snow • *(Third Eye)* • WHITE
Calms and balances the third eye chakra, eases fear of opening one's psychic abilities, teaches how to use new psychic abilities, aids learning to meditate, balances kundalini reactions, promotes gentle opening. *Note:* Snow Quartz provides a softer energy than is found in most Quartz varieties.

Quartz—Spirit (Amethyst) • *(Crown)* • PURPLE
Amplifies Amethyst energy, purifies the crown chakra and Kundalini Line; opens spirituality, transforms by causing sudden new opening and interest in spiritual subjects, causes sudden new psychic opening, opens new psychic abilities for people already on a spiritual path—a beautiful and powerful energy; stabilizes through times of change—deliberate but usually gentle and not frightening in its action. *Note:* Spirit Quartz is also called Cactus Quartz.

Quartz—Spirit (Citrine) • *(Entire Hara Line)* • GOLD-BROWN
Regenerates on all levels; heals, repairs, rewires, reprograms, and reconnects; heals core soul damage; repairs the mind grid and mind grid chakras; repairs and reconnects the DNA; aids regeneration from psychic attacks and all damage and destruction from evil interference; brings in aid for healing from Light Be-ings and protection from the angelic realm; aids healers who do high-level psychic work and who battle evil. *Note:* Spirit Quartz is also called Cactus Quartz.

Quartz—Spirit (Red-Violet)

(Causal Body Chakra) • RED-VIOLET

Develops and opens the causal body chakra so the Light's communication can come in; promotes sensory perception with the Light—psychic hearing, vision, touch, and fragrance; amplifies current psychic abilities and opens new ones; purifies and stabilizes the Hara Line; repairs and balances the Hara Line chakra system; promotes and aids ascension; raises one's personal vibration; furthers spiritual evolution; aids multidimensional travel. *Note:* Spirit Quartz is also called Cactus Quartz.

Quartz—Strawberry • *(Heart)* • PINK AND BLACK

Provides balanced unconditional love for others and oneself, aids giving and receiving, promotes viewing life with understanding and compassion for all; promotes understanding one's past lives as they have influenced this lifetime, promotes understanding this lifetime's place in one's record of many lifetimes and incarnations; opens the heart while grounding one in this lifetime and body, encourages compassion for the not-perfect body, heals the heart, reduces stress, increases joy and self-love. *Note:* Beads sold under this name are very often imitations or dyed glass, so buyers beware.

Quartz—Tangerine • *(Belly)* • PEACH

Stimulates joy, happiness, love for life, and living; inspires laughter including "belly laughs"; aids in seeing the humor in life and lightening up; promotes finding the best in any situation; helps people who are overly serious; promotes emotional and physical relaxation; aids depression and grief.

Quartz—Tourmaline • *(Earth)* • BLACK AND CLEAR

Protects one's life purpose for this incarnation; aids grounding one's life purpose in the earth-plane reality and manifesting it on the earth-plane; aids in keeping one's pre-life agreed-upon karmic contracts and remembering the reasons for one's current incarnation; repels negative energies and entities; provides psychic protection; provides support for honoring one's promises, life agreements, and path.

Quartz—Vogel Crystal • *(Transpersonal Point)* • CLEAR

Cleanses and repairs, provides a template of perfection that brings all energies into perfect form; aligns, rewires, and creates connections; acts as a laser for psychic surgeries—a Light wand; brings in the purest Light and Light Be-ings; connects with the Light; evolves to ascension; raises Light vibration on all levels. This is a superb all-around healer's tool. *Note:* Vogel Quartz is clear Quartz Crystal that is precision cut and polished into twelve, twenty-four, or more faceted sides. Other stones besides clear Quartz Crystal can be cut into Vogel form.

Quartz—White Phantom • *(Transpersonal Point)* • WHITE
Balances Earth Ch'i and Heavenly Ch'i and the entire Hara Line; opens the galactic body chakras beyond the transpersonal point; expands awareness into the Body of Light, mind grid, and planetary grid; opens the aura to the positive aid of other-planetary healers, spirit guides, angels, Goddesses, and Light Beings; balances energy flows through all the Kundalini Line, Hara Line, and all the chakras; expands the aura's ability to hold Light, information, and energy/Ch'i. *Note:* Use these white crystals in pairs or paired with Black Velvet Tourmaline for psychic surgery.

Rainbow Aura Crystal • *(Entire Hara Line)* • IRIDESCENT PURPLE
Aligns, repairs, and heals the entire Hara Line system and its chakras and connections; clears karma and the effects of karma from the Hara Line and the emotional body; aids in working with the Lords of Karma for karmic release, accessing past lives and simultaneous realities; brings past-life issues to awareness for release. *Note:* Quartz Crystal is irradiated with Titanium to produce this crystal, also known as Titanium Quartz.

See also Aqua Aura Crystal, Cobalt Aura Crystal, Opal Aura Crystal, Rose Aura Crystal, and Silver Aura Crystal.

Rainbow Calsilica • *(Entire Kundalini Line)* • MULTI-COLORS
Aligns the kundalini chakras and the first four bodies (physical, emotional, mental, and spiritual); repairs the aura, the chakras, and the four bodies; cleanses and purifies; removes dull spots and debris; brightens, heals, and opens; provides wonderful energy for children as it works gently and with joy; promotes wellness, well-being, happiness, love of life, and creativity. *Note:* Rainbow Calsilica resembles a multicolored sand painting.

Rhodochrosite • *(Heart)* • PINK AND YELLOW

Cleanses the heart chakra and the emotional body of the need to suffer, releases karmic guilt "the Cross of St. Michael," releases suffering from past lives held in the present-life aura, reprograms the emotional body to receive joy, heals the ability to give and receive, heals chronic self-blame, detoxifies the physical and emotional body, eases digestive problems and ulcers.

Rhodochrosite—Gem Crystalline

(Causal Body Chakra) • PEACH AND RED

Heals blocks to spiritual-level energy entering the Hara Line; opens a blocked ability to know and manifest one's life purpose and karmic agreements for this incarnation; heals a lack of connection with the Goddess, lack of spirituality in one's life, and lack of reason for Be-ing; supports people who are dying because they have refused to keep their contracts for this lifetime; prevents the emotional sources of cancer.

Rhodonite • *(Heart)* • PINK AND BLACK

Grounds emotional flights into earth-plane reality, provides support for those who fall in love too fast and too often, helps in recognizing the real from wishful in relationships, aids in seeing one's current flame as a real person; promotes maturity in love affairs and relationships, helps to know real from fantasy in love.

Rhyolite • *See* Jasper—Rainforest.

Rosasite • *(Thymus)* • RUST-BROWN AND AQUA
Stimulates and clears the thymus chakra and the entire Hara Line; heals the emotional body; clears the connection between the heart and thymus chakras, the Hara Line and Kundalini Line; reduces stress, burnout, overstimulation, sensory overload, and being overwhelmed; calms and balances; soothes; aids endurance; boosts the immune system.

Rose Aura Crystal • *(Heart)* • IRIDESCENT PINK
Brings pink Light into the heart chakra, heals one's ability to be open to emotions and to feel safe in experiencing one's emotions and feelings, heals the ability to be open to others and to trust, aids the ability to give and receive, encourages compassion for others and oneself, promotes positive

self-love, heals emotional heart damage, helps to clear heart scars, promotes inner peace and warmth, calms, support for those with heart dis-ease. *Note:* Rose Aura Crystal is made by irradiating and bonding Rose Quartz with silver for a pearly iridescent effect.

See also Aqua Aura Crystal, Cobalt Aura Crystal, Opal Aura Crystal, Rainbow Aura Crystal, Rose Aura Crystal, and Silver Aura Crystal.

Rubellite • *See* Tourmaline—Pink.

Ruby • *(Root and Perineum)* • RED

Intensifies life force energy in the root chakra and the Kundalini Line; connects the Kundalini and Hara Lines at the perineum, thereby connecting one's life force with one's life purpose at the physical level; stimulates the will to live and the body's ability to continue this incarnation; eases physical coldness, weakness, chronic blood dis-eases, chronic fatigue, low vitality, and burnout.

Ruby—Star • *(Causal Body Chakra)* • RED-VIOLET

Brings information and Light into conscious awareness; stimulates contact with spirit guides, angels, positive extra-terrestrials, Light Be-ings, and Goddesses; aids channeling and automatic writing of information from other levels; accesses information from and connection with the mind grid and the Earth grid; aids psychics who spend too much time out of body, stabilizes all levels; supports and aids those with chronic fatigue, weakness, and debility.

Ruby with Black Zoisite • *(Root)* • RED AND BLACK

Combines full connection to the life force of the Earth with balanced grounding, stimulates energy that is centered and calm, provides steady energy refill when exhausted, heals burnout, aid for exhaustion and overdoing; balances and grounds one's energy after psychic work, lights a steady warm flame within, promotes centered peacefulness, sustains one's life force and this incarnation.

Ruby with Fuchsite • *(Diaphragm)* • RED AND GREEN

Aids karmic release of disturbing situations and lifetimes or of past-life violent deaths; brings emotions and their sources into awareness for understanding and clearing; works via flashbacks, nightmares, and daydream images too disturbing and message-laden to ignore; releases and clears emotional garbage to end its influence on one's present life and prevent its carryover into future incarnations. *Note:* Ruby energizes and intensifies Fuchsite's ability to cleanse and purge the emotions. Not always gentle in its action, it is best to use Ruby with Fuchsite in moderation.

Ruby with Zoisite • *(Heart)* • RED AND GREEN
Promotes connection with the Light for healing, trance states, altered states, expanded consciousness with safe grounding, and exploring simultaneous realities; clears the mind; sharpens thinking and an analytical ability; aids in achieving unconditional love; promotes self-awareness; aids healers in their work and helps to prevent healers' burnout; helps in obtaining information for more effective healing for others and oneself; aids self-healing. *Note:* This stone is also called Anyolite.

Saganite • *(Hara Chakra)* • RED-BROWN

Protects the Hara chakra and one's life purpose from attacks and negative entities; protects one's ability to accomplish one's life purpose for this incarnation; stimulates creativity, whether the creation is artistic or bearing children; aids mothers, as the mother's hara protection extends to her unborn and young children; promotes certainty and ease in accomplishing one's life purpose; helps in being a successful parent.

Salmonite • *(Movement)* • TAN AND BEIGE

Clears energy blockages in the knees by healing one's ability to move forward in life and on one's life path; eases resistance to or fear of one's agreed-upon life purpose; heals rigidity and inflexibility on the emotional level; supports the healing of dis-eases of the feet, knees, and legs—numbness, varicose veins, poor circulation, frostbite, knee or foot damage and pain, and arthritic knees. *Note:* Also spelled Sammonite.

Sapphire—Black • *(Earth)* • BLACK

Brings Light and healing through the Hara Line from the transpersonal point to below the feet; aids transformative clearing and activation of one's life purpose—puts one on one's path; aids knowing and understanding what one's life purpose is; establishes a strong desire to accomplish one's life purpose, life goals, and karmic agreements; initiates activations, breakthroughs and transformations; enhances connection with Light Be-ings, spirit guides, and helpers; provides protection on one's life path; provides electrical transformative energy.

Sapphire—Blue • *(Causal Body Chakra)* • INDIGO
Fills the Hara Line with Light; increases communication with, connection to, and awareness of spirit guides, angels, the Goddess, and the Light; promotes development, activation, and opening of the Light Body; cleanses the soul and the mind grid; activates, manifests, and supports one's life purpose and brings it into earth-plane consciousness; focuses one's intent and awareness on fulfilling one's life purpose and karmic agreements; promotes ascension and soul growth; brings gifts of fulfillment into one's life—joy, prosperity, inner peace, and beauty. *Note:* Sapphire is a powerful and transformative gemstone energy that may work quickly and drastically. Most

Sapphires today are lab grown but seem to have all the healing attributes of natural stones.

Sapphire—Natural Star

(Causal Body Chakra) • BLUE AND SILVER

Establishes reception of other-dimensional and other-planetary information for healing oneself and others; promotes becoming a clear channel for healing; provides connection for working with the angelic realm and Light Be-ings in healing; aids teachers of healing and healers; supports people in service to others and the planet; aids in becoming an old soul, becoming a bodhisattva; prevents and heals burnout; serves healers in their own healing needs.

Sapphire—Orange (Jacinth) • *(Hara Chakra)* • ORANGE

Activates the hara chakra and entire Hara Line; stimulates the will to live and the will to achieve one's life purpose; stimulates one's desire for soul growth and for experiences that lead to soul growth; aids in manifesting conditions that facilitate and guide one's life purpose; brings joy and success into one's life; promotes curiosity, sexuality, and creativity.

Sapphire—Pink • *(Heart)* • PINK

Promotes emotional transformation and transformative healing; clears current, past, and past-life emotional pain; promotes emotional release and "crying it out"; clears heart scars; changes anger and resentment into forgiveness and acceptance; encourages heart opening and heart warming; promotes going on after hurts and betrayals, restores trust; heals the emotional body, astral body, and astral twin; clears the silver cord and the chakras on the back. *Note:* Pink Sapphire is gentler than other Sapphires, but it is thorough in its action. Pink Sapphire used to be called Pigeon's Blood Ruby.

Sapphire—Purple • *(Crown)* • PURPLE

Aids spiritual growth and transformation; clears, detoxifies, opens, activates, and aligns the crown chakra, kundalini channels and chakras, etheric body, and etheric double; clears and activates the Ka and Etheric templates; fills the aura with Light; aids in karmic healing, releasing, and repatterning; transforms negativity, energy blocks and obstructions; opens connection to spirit guides, the Goddess and Goddess within; activates spiritual opening and spiritual breakthroughs, the Violet Flame; supports and heals the physical body, brain, and central nervous system. *Note*: This is an intense energy for transformational change in one's life that may work quickly and drastically.

Sapphire—Yellow • *(Hara Chakra)* • GOLD AND YELLOW
Moves one's life force energy through the Hara Line channels and the Ch'i kung microcosmic orbit; expands the hara's ability to hold Earthly and Heavenly Ch'i, increase spiritual energy through the etheric and emotional bodies; intensifies commitment to one's life purpose and karmic agreements; aids in fulfilling one's path; promotes abundance and prosperity; heals burnout, depression, lack of energy, and chronic exhaustion.

Scapolite—Gold • *(Diaphragm)* • YELLOW
Cleanses, purifies, and removes blockages from the diaphragm chakra; removes the emotional garbage that prevents one from moving forward; opens emotional images and flashbacks for clearing and resolving; effects permanent release of old karma and old karmic patterns; ends suffering at

the source, but not always gently; promotes change in every aspect of one's life; promotes moving forward on one's path and in one's life once old issues are removed.

Schorl • *See* Tourmaline—Black.

Scolecite • *(Crown)* • CLEAR AND WHITE

Purifies, clears, and heals the crown chakra; opens the crown chakra and one's connections with the Light; aligns and balances; connects the crown chakra, resulting in oneness, inner peace, and awareness that one is safe, loved, and not alone; brings in the Goddess and the Goddess's love; promotes contact with Light Be-ings, Goddesses, Gods, and the angelic realm; aids meditation, dream work, all psychic work, ascension, and all spirituality.

Sea Glass • *(Chakra Matches Color)* • CLEAR AND COLORS

Promotes awareness of one's connection with all other people and Be-ings, knowing all life is one life; connects with the sea, sea creatures, and ocean Goddesses, according to the element of water; promotes reception of messages from dolphins, whales, and sea turtles; aids knowing that all life comes from the sea; promotes protecting the sea and sea life—water environmentalism; offers knowledge and fond memory of the womb, soothes and calms.

Selenite—Angel Wing • *(Transpersonal Point)* • WHITE
Moves one's energy upward on the Hara Line; fills the Hara Line with Light; aids connection with and channeling of one's spirit guides, angels, the Goddess, and other discarnate helpers and healers; connects with angelic realms and positive other-planetary Be-ings and Light Be-ings; gives a sense of security and a certainty of one's place in the universe; provides knowledge of oneself as far more than this lifetime in this body; provides knowledge of soul structure and between life states, one's soul and Oversoul; repairs DNA, promotes core soul healing; an all-healer, very calming. *Note:* This stone is soft and very fragile.

Selenite—Clear • *(Transpersonal Point)* • CLEAR, WHITE
Opens, aligns and clears the aura bodies; opens energy blocks; fills the aura with Light; transmits Light, information,

and energy (Ch'i); promotes ascension; heals the Light Body; provides connection with the Earth and interspace grids; repairs DNA; promotes the channeling of information from the Pleiades; protects, transforms, and heals negativity.

Selenite—Desert Rose • *(Vision)* • BEIGE AND WHITE
Provides spiritual nourishment; contacts the Mother Goddess; aids feeling cared for, safe, and cared about; promotes knowledge of being taken care of by the universe and the Mother; promotes a sense of security, safety, feeling that all is well, inner peace, and knowing that one is valued in the universal plan; provides emotional support for breast-feeding; helps nursing mothers have enough breast milk; promotes giving nourishment as well as receiving it.

Selenite—Green • *(Diaphragm)* • LIGHT GREEN
Clears and detoxifies the diaphragm chakra by filling and flushing it with Light; clears, frees, and heals the emotional body, astral body, and astral twin; aids in reconnecting full-complement DNA; aids genetic clearing and reprogramming; heals the Light Body; aids in connecting with the Light Body

and in merging it with the astral twin; promotes all ascension processes and the ascension path. *Note:* Green Selenite is delicate and fragile.

Selenite—Hour Glass • *(Hara Chakra)* • CLEAR AND ORANGE
Fits one's life purpose into one's lifetime, promotes fulfillment of one's life goals for this incarnation, aids in completing and manifesting one's life agreements and attaining agreed upon soul growth while there is time to do so, provides awareness of time as a physical limit, stops procrastination, clears the hara chakra and Hara Line channels.

Selenite—Phantom • *(Movement)* • CLEAR AND TAN
Brings spiritual-level knowledge into earth-plane action, connects spirituality to daily life; fills the entire Hara Line and emotional body with Light; clears, balances, and stabilizes all the hara line chakras; supports healing for neurological dis-eases, injuries and traumas, and strokes; supports healing for insomnia, nightmares, and night terrors; calms, balances, stabilizes, heals, and soothes.

Septarian—Brown • *(Grounding)* • BROWN, BLACK

Promotes the ability for a one-pointed earth-plane focus; aids doing one thing at a time and completing it before going on to something else; helps to reduce procrastination and putting things off; grounds scattered and diffused energy; aids moving forward on one's path in a self-directed and focused way; promotes certainty of one's path on the earth-plane; calms, grounds, and centers. *Note:* Another name for Septarian is Septerye.

Septarian—Yellow • *(Solar Plexus)* • YELLOW AND TAN

Opens the solar plexus chakra for concentrated energy intake, assimilation, and one-pointed focus; takes in energy and psychic information from and about other people when they are focused upon, whether they are physically present or not; directs concentrated psychic focus; aids nonverbal and psychic communication between people; reduces distraction and scattering of mental energy; increases psychic impressions and information; aids psychic healers, psychic readers, and tarot readers. *Note:* Another name for Septarian is Septerye.

Seraphanite • *(Vision)* • GREY AND SILVER

Aligns the soul bodies; opens and aligns the Light Body to the astral body vibration; harmonizes energy vibration rates among the bodies and chakras; brings one's astral twin self into the physical-level aura; purifies the aura; promotes contact with spirit guides, angels, and the Goddess; invokes protection, help, healing and love; promotes awareness of one's place in the universal plan, psychic vision, and spiritualized seeing of the world; promotes peace in the world and in oneself. *Note:* Seraphanite is sometimes called Serafina.

Serpentine • *(Diaphragm)* • LIGHT GREEN

Clears, develops, and expands the Hara Line's ability to hold energy; detoxifies and clears the hara chakras and Hara Line of blockages; aids grounding and cleansing; moves energy in a strong downward stream that may not be comfortable. *Note:* This is not a major healing energy in its raw form.

Serpentine Jade • *(Heart)* • LIGHT GREEN

Opens the heart as a leaf opens in spring; supports gentle opening; inspires trust; aids learning to love or to love again after heartbreak; promotes reaching out to others; supports new love and new lovers; encourages learning to love and validate oneself; provides emotional healing and unfolding; aids first love—especially good for women and youths; protects vulnerability; supports feeling emotionally safe enough to love and trust. *Note:* This stone is also called New Jade.

Serpentine Jade—Olivine • *(Solar Plexus)* • YELLOW GREEN
Heals the heart and solar plexus to bring emotions into the physical level for release; heals the emotions that cause physical disease; heals the body via the heart; releases old hurts; clears anger, envy, greed, jealousy and vengefulness, and changes them to love and peace; supports the digestion and kidney function. *Note:* Also called Olivine, Olivine New Jade, or Olive Jade, this stone is a form of Serpentine Jade. It is not to be confused with Peridot, which is also called Olivine.

Shaman Stone • *See* Moqui Marbles.

Shattuckite • *(Thymus)* • BLUE-GREEN
Heals the thymus chakra, silver cord, and chakras on the

back; heals the astral body and astral twin; heals soul fragmentation and aids core soul healing; aids in healing past abuse and releasing it from emotional and physical levels; connects one's personal healing with the planet's healing; detoxifies; builds the immune system; supports lung healing; brings hope and optimism; calms; heals deep grief; helps with headaches and migraines; promotes channeling and automatic writing; removes writer's block and psychic blockages to information and creativity; aids connection with the Light and Light guidance; promotes psychic hearing, psychic opening, and enhancement; aids clarity of psychic information and obtaining psychic truth.

Shiva Lingam • *(Perineum)* • BROWN AND RED

Raises and grounds the kundalini; connects the Kundalini and Hara Lines; promotes grounding into one's incarnation and the body; promotes the union of body and soul, male and female; aids sexuality and sexual healing for men and women; promotes transformation and creation. *Note:* Lingams honor the Hindu God Shiva and Hindu Goddess Kali; Shiva is considered to be male but was originally female. Lingams are generally seen as representing the penis, male sexuality, and the male God aspect; they can also be perceived as the egg or seed and female Goddess in form.

Siberian Quartz—Blue • *(Third Eye)* • BLUE-VIOLET
Activates the third eye at higher energy levels and in bodies higher than the first four (physical, emotional, mental, and spiritual); promotes ascension by healing and bringing in the Energy Selves and the Spirit; joins the spirit and soul to the body; promotes psychic work of all kinds—healing, channeling, and obtaining true psychic information; promotes awareness of where we came from; promotes joining with the Goddess and the Light; cleanses and purifies; raises energy vibration; dissolves old karma and karmic patterns; works as an all-healer. *Note:* Siberian Quartz is a Russian lab-grown crystal with strong healing energy. Unlike most lab-grown gems, it works well after precision faceting, but it is quite expensive.

Siberian Quartz—Citrine • *(Solar Plexus)* • GOLD
Cleanses the soul structure on a higher level than at the levels of the known four bodies (physical, emotional, mental,

and spiritual); focuses on the mental levels and the mind grid; repairs, heals, purifies, and reprograms the mind grid at all levels including the creational levels; raises an individual's Light vibration to ascension and beyond; reprograms brain, mind, DNA, spirit and soul; aids in bringing in a Goddess, God, or Family of Light; promotes being one with the Light; activates the Light. *Note:* Siberian Quartz is a Russian lab-grown crystal with strong healing energy. Unlike most lab-grown gems, it works well after precision faceting, but it is quite expensive.

Siberian Quartz—Clear • *(Transpersonal Point)* • CLEAR
Aids all healing; purifies all Light and brings in the Light; raises energy vibrations to ascension level and beyond; activates the bodies, chakras, and templates at the Causal Body level and beyond; repairs, heals and reconnects chakras, bodies, and templates; heals the soul structure; promotes experience of the highest-level Light Be-ings and Goddesses; promotes the ability to join with a Goddess and Family of Light; activates highest-level protection from the angelic realm. *Note:* Siberian Quartz is a Russian lab-grown crystal with strong

healing energy. Unlike most lab-grown gems, it works well after precision faceting, but it is quite expensive.

Siberian Quartz—Green • *(Heart)* • GREEN
Activates the heart chakra at higher energy levels and in bodies higher than the first four (physical, emotional, mental and spiritual); promotes ascension and full DNA connection; promotes connection with the Light; furthers learning unconditional love; promotes service to the Goddess; provides angelic protection; promotes bringing in a Goddess, God or Family of Light; aids karmic purification; aids self-healing. *Note:* Siberian Quartz is a Russian lab-grown crystal with strong healing energy. Unlike most lab-grown gems, it works well after precision faceting, but it is quite expensive.

Siberian Quartz—Purple • *(Crown)* • PURPLE
Activates the crown chakra at higher energy levels and in bodies higher than the first four (physical, emotional, mental, and spiritual); promotes spirituality and spiritual skills on every level; promotes ascension; aids connection with the Light; aids in bringing in a Goddess, God or Family of Light; creates

oneness and being one with the Light. *Note:* Siberian Quartz is a Russian lab-grown crystal with strong healing energy. Unlike most lab-grown gems, it works well after precision faceting, but it is quite expensive.

Siberite • *See* Tourmaline—Violet.

Silicified Saltstone • *(Belly)* • ORANGE AND TAN

Aids meditating upon and understanding the soul's herstory and one's past-life herstory on the Earth; promotes past-life regression, both guided and spontaneous; aids in healing past and present emotional damage; supports incest recovery; helps to heal a woman's reproductive system; eases menarche, menstruation, and menopause; balances hormones; stimulates whole-body self-healing.

Silver Aura Crystal

(Transpersonal Point) • CLEAR AND IRIDESCENT

Fills the auric envelope with Light at the etheric and astral body levels, heals the etheric and emotional body aura, repairs energy tears; strengthens auric protection, protects the aura from other people's negative energy and psychic attacks, clears negative energy from the aura but not from the chakras. *Note:* Silver Aura Crystal is made by irradiating and bonding Clear Quartz Crystal with silver.

See also Aqua Aura Crystal, Cobalt Aura Crystal, Opal Aura Crystal, Rainbow Aura Crystal, Rose Aura Crystal.

Smithsonite—Aqua • *(Thymus)* • AQUA
Aids opening oneself to repressed emotions in order to clear and heal them; heals grief, rage, anger, resentment, sadness, sorrow, and heartache; supports the release process and gentles it, heals the fear of one's own strong emotions; speeds the releasing; refills the aura with peace, healing and security.

Smithsonite—Pink • *(Heart)* • PINK
Promotes trusting others and oneself; promotes trusting the Goddess; aids opening up to let others in, letting down walls that block one's heart growth and joy; promotes opening the heart, learning to love and give to others, and releasing resentment and blame; promotes forgiving others and oneself.

Soapstone • *(Vision)* • WHITE
Aids visualization; promotes the ability to see the finished figure in the lump of stone; aids creativity and sculpting; promotes creating a visualized reality, making a dream come alive through artistry and expertise; guides artists to their highest potential; helps working with the hands and finishing the projects one begins.

Sodalite • *(Third Eye)* • BLUE AND WHITE
Balances the pituitary gland and the third eye chakra; supports healing for the lymphatic and glandular systems, nerve endings, vision nerves, and central nervous system; promotes beginning psychic vision; helps new psychics to accept opening; calms fear of one's psychic vision and abilities; aids in letting go of control and trusting the Goddess and the process; soothes and heals; stabilizes.

Sphalerite • *(Earth)* • BLACK
Supports other-planetary souls now in Earth bodies; helps one to feel a part of life on this planet; helps one to feel like she belongs here; eases loneliness, alienation from others and society,

feeling different and isolated, and homesickness for one's star home; eases environmental illnesses; promotes grounding.

Spinel—Red • *(Perineum)* • RED

Aligns the etheric and emotional aura bodies; connects the Kundalini and Hara Lines; rejuvenates, regenerates, and detoxifies the etheric double aura; lengthens life by balancing Ch'i energy and removing blocks to energy flow; brings Earth Ch'i into the body; stimulates the Ch'i kung microcosmic orbit through the aura electrical system; accesses the gateway of life and death, incarnation and reincarnation; promotes physical vitality; refills spent energy; eases exhaustion.

Sponge—Fossilized • *(Crown)* • LAVENDER

Holds the memories of the evolution of the seas, all sea life forms, and the origins of life from the seas; supports people who work with whales, dolphins, mermaids, sea spirits, sea life, and sea environments; promotes psychic communication with sea life-forms and Be-ings; aids learning from the sea, understanding element of water. *Note:* All fossils contain records of the ancient past.

Staurolite (Fairy Cross) • *(Vision)* • GREY AND BLACK

For seeing the world as the fairies and "little people" see it; promotes seeing nature devas, Earth elementals, water spirits, tree spirits, aids working co-creatively with the unseen world; good for gardeners, flower essence therapists, crystal healers; enlists the help of Earth spirits and Mother Earth; for healing with the aid of nature and the planet; honors the four directions, as above so below, protects from the "evil eye."

Stichtite • *(Causal Body Chakra)* • RED-VIOLET

Stimulates the development and opening of the causal body chakra at the base of the skull; promotes psychic reception, information, channeling, and hearing; aids development of the Hara Line system chakras; aids opening the chakras on the back of the body; promotes ascension and connection with the Light, reconnection of DNA, and advanced psychic abilities; raises awareness and one's energy vibration.

Stilbite—Orange • *(Hara Chakra)* • ORANGE AND CLEAR

Connects the transpersonal point chakra to the hara chakra, bringing in energy as information through the whole Hara

Line; promotes psychic knowing, guidance, and direction; provides information on the soul, soul structure, and spiritual realities; promotes core soul healing of the abilities to receive spiritual energy and information from the Light; accesses the Akashic Records; increases Heavenly Ch'i; clears and cleanses the hara chakra.

Stilbite—Pink • *(Heart)* • PINK AND CLEAR
Heals present, past. and past-life heart hurts and emotional pain; heals past abuse and its damage in this life and past lives; releases heart scars gently; connects the Hara and Kundalini Lines; clears and opens the Hara Line channels; heals the emotional body, astral body, and astral twin; aids core soul healing and reconnection of full complement DNA; reprograms karma for heart healing; brings information about the soul and healing one's soul; fills the etheric, emotional, mental, and spiritual bodies with Light and healing.

Stromatolite • *(Entire Hara Line)* • SAND COLORS
Record keeper of who we are and where we have been; contains the herstory of the Earth and herstory of Earth life, keeps

a record of planetary DNA; use it to meditate on the planet and the development of life on Earth; use it to meditate on one's own herstory going back to the planet's genesis, contains a record of all one's past lives; opens the Akashic Records of individuals and the Earth. *Note:* This gemstone is a fossilized sedimentary sand formation.

Sugilite • *(Crown)* • PURPLE AND BLACK
Opens, clears, and balances the kundalini channels and kundalini chakras; helps a spiritual person live well on the earth-plane; cushions the Earth's harshness for spiritually oriented people; aids living in the present rather than dwelling on the past or future; transcends the limits of time; heals the body via the mind and karmic healing; offers connection to creation, the Non-Void, and the Goddess within; tunes one's personal vibration to that of the Earth and the planetary mind grid; releases and heals despair, hostility, and discouragement; balances the brain's left and right hemispheres; eases dyslexia, strokes, and epilepsy.

Sulfur • *(Diaphragm)* • YELLOW

Detoxifies the physical body of dis-eases with emotional origins, heals karmic dis-eases by releasing their source in this life or in past lifetimes; focuses primarily on dis-eases that originated in the past and carried over from other lifetimes; supports those with skin conditions, asthma, and lung dis-eases. *Note:* Do not soak this stone in water, as the mineral will dissolve.

Sunstone—Orange • *(Hara Chakra)* • ORANGE-GOLD

Clears blockages in the hara chakra, supports the life force and the Hara Line; clears impediments to fulfilling one's life purpose, helps in completing karmic contracts and manifesting one's life purpose on the earth-plane, promotes courage, heals fear, offers a candle of hope in the darkness.

Sunstone—Yellow • *(Solar Plexus)* • GOLDEN

Aids worldly success; promotes courage in school, work or business; aids prosperity; helps in finding a job and keeping it; promotes success in business, school or work; facilitates organizational ability, mental clarity, self-confidence, alertness, good work or study habits, and intuition in business and finance; aids and promotes the ability to receive and assimilate ideas and energy from the Light; stimulates the intellect.

Tanzanite • *(Causal Body Chakra)* • BLUE-VIOLET

Opens the causal body chakra to make new spiritual awareness possible; cleanses the emotional body at the spiritual chakra levels; promotes an interest in metaphysics, spirituality and psychic work; opens an awareness of the comparison between how one lives and how one could *choose* to live more consciously; opens consciousness and awareness; aids in spiritually influenced life choices; promotes manifesting a spiritual lifestyle.

Tektite • *(Earth)* • BLACK

Expands, aligns, and clears all the kundalini chakras and the Kundalini Line; connects the Kundalini and Hara Lines; protects energy; aids in grounding in Earth reality; promotes safety and security; brings in positive help from non-Earth Light Be-ing sources; promotes connection and communication with Pleiadian healers and planetary protectors; makes one a channel for extraterrestrial help for the planet; protects the aura against negative alien interference; aids in removing negative energy implants.

Tempest Stone • *See* Pietersite.

Thulite • *(Root)* • RED

Moves Earth energy upward through the kundalini chakras; balances and clears the chakras; aids being rooted in a grounded personal reality; aids manifesting one's life purpose; promotes steadiness, humility, and a balanced ego; recognition of oneself as a part of all life; supports and balances a woman's reproductive system, premenstrual syndrome, and intestinal and bowel dis-eases.

Thunder Egg

Another name for Geode. *See* Agate—Geode.

Tiger Eye—Black or Blue • *See* Hawk's Eye.

Tiger Eye—Golden • *(Solar Plexus)* • GOLD AND BROWN

Makes one invisible to negative energy sources, offers protection against psychic attacks, clears negative energy from the solar plexus, returns negative energy to its sender, traditionally used to protect travelers and automobiles from accidents, protects from things without, aids one's ability to discern evil, supports physical vision.

Tiger Eye—Red • *(Perineum)* • RED AND BROWN

Connects the Kundalini and Hara Lines at the root and perineum chakras, aids in drawing Earth energy into the body and chakra system, starts the flow of the Ch'i kung microcosmic orbit through the Hara Line, increases life force energy through the hara channels, raises the kundalini, offers protection.

Tiger Iron (Tiger Eye with Hematite)

(Solar Plexus) • BROWN AND BLACK

Promotes grounding, reduces stress by decreasing one's psychic sensitivity, offers psychic protection in war and danger, shields and closes the solar plexus chakra by grounding its energy into the Earth, brings one back to Earth from channeling or psychic work, eases psychic hypersensitivity to city noise and pollution, reduces psychic overload, repels negative psychic energies from other people, helps those who take on others' emotions in crowds, a good stone for men and those whose new psychic opening is still ungrounded and untrained, aids focusing on the here and now, stops daydreaming, helps in finding and keeping a job. *Note:* This energy is best used only when needed; it should not be worn all the time. It is never good to refuse one's psychic abilities on any ongoing basis.

Tinguaite • *(Heart)* • DARK GREEN
Promotes serenity; calms the heart and emotions; provides acceptance of what must be; heals grief, loss, and heartbreak; aids acceptance of serious or terminal dis-eases whether for oneself or a loved one; promotes understanding of the karma involved in suffering physical or emotional pain; helps one to recover emotionally from material loss; provides the courage, peace, and strength to continue, end or start over.

Topaz—Blue • *(Throat)* • LIGHT BLUE

Aids in feeling one's anger and releasing it, promotes understanding and feeling one's emotions and emotional pain, supports learning one's true and real feelings and honoring them, aids letting go of anger and resentment, aids surrendering to forgiveness of oneself and others, promotes turning one's pain over to the Goddess and the Light for healing.

Topaz—Champagne • *(Movement)* • BEIGE OR TAN

Brings spiritual-level (Hara Line) energy into earth-plane manifestation, promotes energy movement from the head to the feet, causes life changes and gentle transformations, transforms spiritual path inertia into Earth level physical movement, promotes commitment to and fulfillment of karmic pre-life agreements and one's life purpose, ends procrastination for action and change, holds one to one's life path.

Topaz—Clear or White • *(Transpersonal Point)* • CLEAR

Brings the energy of life change and transformation into the emotional body; initiates a time of change and transition, positive breakthroughs, growth, karmic clearing, and soul healing;

promotes sudden shifts in one's energy balance but otherwise works gently; releases negative entities and attachments.

Topaz—Golden • *(Solar Plexus)* • YELLOW

Stabilizes all life changes and transitions from birth to death; heals the etheric double aura; balances energy flows through the central nervous system; balances the alignment of body, mind and emotions on all levels; clears and heals the Light Body; promotes reincarnation while in the body (total karmic life change); stabilizes deep healing work and aura repair; protects the aura during transformations; promotes detoxification; supports and heals the sacral-cranial spinal rhythm.

Tourmaline—Black • *(Earth)* • BLACK

Protects the aura and this incarnation, brings Earth energy into the root chakra and the kundalini channels, provides a protective shield, absorbs and transmutes negative energy and negative thought forms from oneself and others, offers protection from psychic attacks and spirit possessions, eases fear and panic and promotes a sense of safety and security;

activates the ability to ground and center, aids being rooted into the Earth and the physical body; promotes feeling welcome on the earth-plane, aids the ability to stay in the body. *Note:* Black Tourmaline is also called Schorl.

Tourmaline—Black Velvet • *(Earth)* • BLACK
Opens and balances the Hara Line and all the hara chakras; provides a vibrating energy that expands, aligns, and opens energy blocks, heals obstructions that keep one's life purpose from being manifested; roots this incarnation's life agreements into physical achievement; aids connection to Earth Ch'i for nurturance from the planet; provides entrance to the creational Void and Non-Void for releasing limitations and negative karma; promotes grounding and centering, security, and stability.

Tourmaline—Blue • *(Thymus)* • BLUE-GREEN
Opens and clears the thymus chakra; connects the Hara Line and the emotional body to the Kundalini Line and the etheric body channels; cleanses and stabilizes the Hara Line and hara chakras; transforms emotional healing into

physical healing of dis-ease; focuses one's life purpose on service to the planet and people; fosters the desire and dedication to fulfill one's life path and purpose; protects the full aura and one's life purpose; aids those who give too much to also be able to receive; aids living the Bodhisattva Vow in a balanced way; aids, protects, and balances healers; promotes energy flow through the central nervous system. *Note:* Blue Tourmaline is also called Indicolite.

Tourmaline—Clear or Colorless

(Transpersonal Point) • CLEAR AND SILVER

Provides all-aura protection and all-aura clearing; promotes contact and communication with positive extraterrestrial Beings, Light Be-ings, spirit guides, angels, and ascended healers; aids channeling, automatic writing, and all psychic abilities; clears and energizes the hara line and kundalini channels; repairs full-complement DNA; heals core soul damage; promotes karmic grace and ascension; fills all the levels with information and Light; an all-healer. *Note:* Clear or Colorless Tourmaline is also called Achroite; it is a rare stone.

Tourmaline—Green • *(Diaphragm)* • GREEN

Opens and drains the diaphragm chakra; purges and releases negative emotions from the Hara Line and one's life purpose, clears the emotional body of past-life and present-life traumas and negative emotional patterns; protects while one is going through the detoxification process; offers aura insulation, safety, and trust while detoxifying, detoxifies the aura and chakras at the physical etheric and emotional levels; supports clearing the gall bladder and liver at the emotional level. *Note:* Green Tourmaline is also called Verdelite; it is the most common of the Tourmaline gemstone colors. It is deep acting and fast acting, and it can cause intense releases; use it moderately.

Tourmaline—Pink • *(Causal Body Chakra)* • RED-VIOLET

Provides deeply comforting love energy; opens and heals the entire emotional body; brings one's life purpose into all the hara chakras and into earth-plane conscious awareness; balances energy flow in the hara line and kundalini channels and chakras; removes blockages and negativity from the whole aura and chakra system at all levels; transforms negativity into positive emotional energy; fills the emotional body and etheric body channels and chakras with Light, information, peace, joy, and universal love; promotes compassion for oneself and others and a lifetime of service; supports those on the bodhisattva path. *Note:* Pink Tourmaline is also called Rubellite.

Tourmaline—Violet • *(Crown)* • PURPLE

Protects against, prevents, and clears spirit attachments, negative entities, spirit possession, and low level entities; protects and releases negative alien implants and interference; clears the human energy system at etheric, emotional, mental, and Light Body levels of negative violations from this life only (will not heal those brought in from past lifetimes); fills the Kundalini and Hara Line channels, chakras, and aura bodies with Light. *Note:* Violet Tourmaline is also called Siberite.

Tourmaline—Watermelon • *(Heart)* • PINK AND GREEN

Heals and opens one's ability to reach out to others; promotes trust of self, others, life, and the Goddess; promotes self-love and unconditional love; encourages service to the planet; aids wounded healers; eases past abuse; heals and removes heart scars; brings one's prelife karmic agreements and life purpose into one's heart; opens the heart chakra and the causal body chakra to receive and feel the Light's love. *Note:* Jewelers call this stone Multi-Colored Tourmaline.

Tremolite • *(Vision)* • SILVER
Promotes visualization and visualized imagery for healing and manifesting, connects and activates the vision chakras behind the eyes (Hara Line), connects the vision chakras to the Kundalini third eye, aids psychic healing work, aids using the eyes as lasers for psychic surgery, aids "seeing into" others motives and needs. *Note:* Tremolite is also called Natural Cat's Eye.

Tsavorite • *See* Garnet—Yellow-Green (Grossularite); sometimes used commercially in place of Moldavite.

Turquoise—African • *(Movement)* • GREEN AND BROWN
African Turquoise is not Turquoise, but dyed Jasper. It is less expensive than Turquoise and is often used commercially as a substitute.

Turquoise—Blue • *(Thymus)* • AQUA

Opens, clears, and develops the thymus chakra; connects the Kundalini and Hara Line channels at the thymus and throat chakras; heals present-life and past-life blocks in the throat chakra; opens, heals, and releases present-life and past-life fear and grief; heals sadness about one's life and deeds; heals karmic and present-life shame and guilt; connects physical and spiritual awareness; develops inner strength and calm; stabilizes; heals the emotions and the emotional body; promotes communication and creativity; traditionally used for protection, supports the immune system. *Note:* The Native American name for Turquoise is Sky-Stone because it connects the lower and higher chakras, the Above and Below.

Turquoise—Green • *(Heart)* • AQUA-GREEN

Protects, stabilizes, and calms; balances the entire Kundalini Line; operates as a link between the lower and higher kundalini chakras, "as Above so Below"; shields the emotions; heals heartache and heartbreak; supports the physical heart; traditionally used for protection. *Note:* This stone is similar in energy to Blue Turquoise but with a stronger heart and Kundalini Line affinity.

Turquoise—Yellow • *(Heart)* • YELLOW-GREEN

Opens and softens hardness of heart; heals people who say they will not love again; promotes trust, compassion for oneself and others, friendship, and relationships—doesn't go so far as to promote romantic love but may lead to it; heals mother issues; helps in learning to be a mother and to be nurturing. *Note:* Actually Yellow-Green Jasper is this stone's commercial name.

Turritella • *See* Fossil—Turritella.

Ulexite (TV Stone) • *(Vision)* • CLEAR

Inspires and stimulates visual imagery, visions, and information from other dimensions and planets—a window on new and other worlds; promotes the ability to create and heal by visualization; aids willed transformations of reality; creates new opportunities and realities by being able to see them then to make them real; aids manifesting and precision in manifesting. *Note:* Ulexite is also called TV Stone.

Unakite • *(Diaphragm)* • PINK AND GREEN
Clears the diaphragm chakra of toxic emotions and old pain; changes anger, resentment, and vengeance to a positive conscious awareness for clearing; makes negative emotions abhorrent; forces transformation of negativity through awareness; fosters realization of the oneness of all life; promotes compassion.

Ussingite • *(Causal Body Chakra)* • RED-VIOLET
Activates the causal body chakra for receiving the Light; contacts and communicates with Light Be-ings, Goddess, and the angelic realm; aids channeling, clairaudience (psychic hearing), and automatic writing; promotes the feeling of being loved and cared for because of one's connection to the Light; provides awareness of guidance, awareness that one is loved and not alone, and awareness of divine help and protection; promotes serenity, peace, unconditional love, and joy.

Vanadinite • *(Belly)* • ORANGE
Provides emotional support for women's physical healing; eases endometriosis, uterine fibroids, and other tumors;

balances women's reproductive hormones; helps complete uterine lining clearing in menstruation; balances menopause symptoms; regulates menstrual cycles; eases premenstrual syndrome; brings on menses.

Variscite • *(Diaphragm)* • LIME GREEN AND WHITE
Mild detoxifier of negative energy; stabilizes emotional release and healing from the diaphragm chakra, eases nausea and overwhelm from heavy detoxification and energy release, stabilizes the Hara Line after major healing work, heals the "gutted fish" feeling after some healings, helps to clear anesthetics and drugs from the energy bodies, helps to repair aura tears after anesthetics and surgeries, aids postoperative nausea by cleansing and healing the aura.

Verdelite • *See* Tourmaline—Green.

Verdite • *(Heart)* • GREEN
Matches, synchronizes, and stimulates the electrical vibration patterns of the heart and nervous system; balances internal rhythms and magnetism for the heart; clears and supports

the heart chakra and the physical heart rhythm; stimulates kundalini channel energy flow though the heart; promotes calcium balance in the body; supports and balances heart arrhythmias by balancing the heart chakra.

Vesuvianite—Green • *(Heart)* • GREEN
Heals the emotional heart and one's zest for life; opens the heart to joy; lifts depression and a lack of desire for living; promotes the courage to open to love and change; draws prosperity and abundance; support for those with poor blood circulation, high blood pressure, anemia, and heart dis-ease. *Note:* Also called Idocrase, this is a form of volcanic glass that becomes a rich translucent green when polished.

Vesuvianite—Pink • *(Heart)* • PINK
Heals the heart of giving up and of losing the will to live; restores joy, peacefulness, gentleness, unconditional love, and self-love; lifts depression and feelings of uselessness and being unwanted; draws love into one's life; makes one ready to love or love again; ends all need for revenge, hate, envy, and jealousy; heals self-hate. *Note*: Also called Idocrase, this is a form of volcanic glass.

Vesuvianite—Purple • *(Crown)* • PURPLE
Heals energetic imbalances of the mind and brain, balances the brain's right and left sides, furthers psychic opening and development, clears negative thinking processes, ends negative thought forms, revises how one thinks about oneself and one's life, restores hopefulness, restores positive thinking, promotes a positive outlook to make for a happier and healthier life. *Note:* Also called Vesuvianite Sugilite or Idocrase, this is a form of volcanic glass.

Vivianite • *(Earth)* • WHITE, GREY, BLACK
Clears the mind grid and the mental body of negative thoughts and old programming, clears the tendency to see the worst in any situation, promotes positivity and optimism, aids psychic and physical communication by creating a positive and receptive attitude, amplifies the positive and reduces the negative; offers the feeling that Earth is not such a bad place to be.

Volcanic Glass • *See* Obsidian and Vesuvianite.

Wavellite • *(Diaphragm)* • LIGHT GREEN

Prepares the diaphragm chakra for opening and for the ability to clear the emotional body, promotes a readiness to heal emotional issues from this life and past lives, strengthens one emotionally to be able to heal and change; strengthens the diaphragm chakra's functioning ability to initiate and complete a detoxification process, aids emotional clearing at core soul levels.

Wonderstone • *(Belly)* • ORANGE AND TAN

Finds the positive pictures and images stored in the belly chakra; heals the wounded inner child; promotes appreciating the diversity and wonder of life on Earth and of one's own life in this physical body; aids seeing the benefits, positivity, or learning in any situation; stimulates curiosity, seeing the world through a child's eyes. *Note:* Most belly chakra gemstones release stored negative images for clearing; Wonderstone opens and reinforces good memories and the positive.

Wulfenite • *(Belly)* • ORANGE

Warms and energetically cleanses the uterus; promotes hormonal balance, brings on menstruation and promotes flow and full emptying of the uterus; clears the uterus after abortion, miscarriage, or childbirth; stabilizes sexual energy and sexuality; brings order out of confusion in relationships.

Zebra Stone • *(Earth)* • BLACK AND WHITE
Balances the spiritual with the physical, grounds the Above into the Below, raises the Below to access the Above, and merges the Light into the physical body, creates an awareness of one's place in the universal plan, grounds and uplifts simultaneously, aids spiritual evolution and activation, develops the added DNA strands to raise one's Light to ascension levels while living incarnate on Earth, aids excessive spiritual opening and hypersensitivity, provides a psychic filter and protection, stabilizes energy, moves energy downward through the Hara Line for grounding.

Zincite—Clear • *(Transpersonal Point)* • CLEAR
Forcefully opens the transpersonal point and crown chakras for spiritual and psychic opening; removes blocks; repairs, heals, rewires, and reconnects; promotes connection with the Light and Light Be-ings; promotes channeling and all psychic

abilities, functions and knowledge; puts one on a spiritual path or greatly intensifies and accelerates one already on the path; initiates transformations, breakthroughs, and major life changes; promotes ascension; not a subtle energy. *Note:* Zincite is often intense in its actions; use it in moderation.

Zincite—Green • *(Movement)* • LIME GREEN
Promotes transformation, pushes one forward on one's life path, ends procrastination and laziness, promotes urgency to accomplish what one came here to do in this incarnation, puts one on the spiritual path of service to others and the Goddess, provides a spiritual "kick the pants," strong energizer and activator, removes blockages forcefully; promotes forward movement, puts one on the path to ascension, keeps one evolving and progressing toward ever-greater Light. *Note:* Zincite is often intense in its actions; use it in moderation.

Zincite—Orange • *(Hara Chakra)* • RED AND GOLD
Causes forceful transformation in the fires of change for spiritual and karmic growth; refines dross into gold through wisdom; aids fulfilling karmic agreements and one's life

purpose; provides good energy for walk-ins; promotes reincarnation in the physical body in this lifetime; promotes deep spiritual purification, cleanses and clears the emotional body, hara chakras, and entire Hara Line; stimulates energy. *Note:* Zincite is often intense in its actions; use it in moderation.

Zincite—Red • *(Perineum)* • RED

Brings the life force into the body with forceful bursts of red-hot energy; makes one emotionally alive; restores energy; promotes the will to live; promotes activity; clears indolence, laziness, procrastination, depression, and indecision; provides a spiritual "kick in the pants" to get one moving; puts one on one's life path; transforms; promotes breakthroughs for major life changes. *Note:* Zincite is often intense in its actions; use it in moderation.

Zincite—Yellow • *(Hara Chakra)* • YELLOW

Initiates forceful transformation; establishes one's life purpose and puts one on the path; causes sudden change, breakthroughs, and removal of blockages; promotes the end of waiting, procrastination, laziness, and not knowing how to proceed or where to start; aids forceful starts and momentum; aids manifestation of one's life purpose; clears all that prevents or holds one back from manifesting one's life path. *Note:* Zincite is often intense in its actions; use it in moderation.

Zircon—Clear • *(Transpersonal Point)* • CLEAR
Holds all the colors of the rainbow for appreciation of all peoples and cultures; reminds us of the oneness of all life; aids in overcoming racism and ethnocentrism; encourages becoming a global citizen; aids overcoming the damage done to one's emotional body from being discriminated against through racism, ablism, homophobia, or misogyny; heals victimization; promotes positive self-love, love for others, and respect for all.

Zoisite • *See* Ruby with Zoisite and Ruby with Black Zoisite.

INDEX *of* STONES

A

achroite 2
actinolite 2
aegerine 2
afghanite 3
agate—banded 3
agate—black 3
agate—blue lace 4
agate—Botswana (brown) 4
agate—Botswana (pink) 5
agate—bull's-eye 5
agate—cathedral 5
agate—colorin 6
agate—dendritic 6
agate—fairborn 6
agate—fire 7
agate—geode 7
agate—green 8
agate—holly blue 8
agate—leopard skin 8
agate—luna 9
agate—moss or Montana 9
agate—pitayo cactus 10
agate—plume 10
agate—red-brown 11
agate—red lace 11
agate—sand cast 11
agate—sunset 12
agate—Thompsonite eye 12
agate—tree 12
ajoite 13
alum 13
amazonite—aqua 14
amazonite—Russian 14
amber—black 15
amber—cherry 15
amber—copal 16
amber—golden 16
amber—green 17
amber—honey 17
amblygonite 18
amethyst—Brazilian or Mexican 18
amethyst—Canadian 18
amethyst—Canadian with hematite 19
amethyst—chevron 19
amethyst—elestial 20
amethyst—green 20
amethyst—pink 20
amethyst—rutile 21
amethyst—scepter 21
amethyst—smoky 22
ametrine 22
ammonite 22
andalusite 23
Andean opal—blue 23
Andean opal—green 24

Andean opal—pink 24
angelite 24
anhydrite—blue 25
anhydrite—blue druzy 25
anhydrite—purple 26
anyolite 26
Apache gold 26
apatite—blue 27
apatite—yellow 27
Aphrodite 28
apophyllite—aqua 28
apophyllite—black 28
apophyllite—clear 29
apophyllite—golden with celestite 29
apophyllite—green 30
apophyllite—red 30
aqua aura crystal 31
aquamarine 31
aragonite 32
aragonite—banded 32
aragonite—blue 32
astrophyllite 33
atlantisite 33
aurichalcite 34
avalonite (blue druzy chalcedony) 34
aventurine—blue 35
aventurine—green 35
aventurine—peach 36
aventurine—red 36
azurite 36
azurite-malachite 37

B

barite—green 38
barite—peach 38
beryl—golden 38
biotite lens 39
bismuth 39
black onyx 39
blackstone 40
blister pearl 40
bloodstone 40
Boji stone 41
bornite 41
bronzite 41
brookite 42

C

calcite—amber or honey 42
calcite—blue 43
calcite—Brushy Creek 43
calcite—clear lemon 43
calcite—dogtooth 44
calcite—green 44
calcite—mangano 45
calcite—optical 45

calcite—orange 45
calcite—orange-banded 46
calcite—pink 46
calcite—ram's horn 47
calcite—red phantom 47
calcite—white snow 47
calsilica—rainbow 48
carnelian 48
carnelian—poppy 48
cavansite 49
celestite—blue 49
celestite—brown 50
cerussite 50
chalcanthite 51
chalcedony—blue 51
chalcedony—blue druzy 51
chalcedony—brown 52
chalcedony—pink 52
chalcedony—white 52
chalcopyrite 53
chalcotrichite 53
charoite 54
chiastolite andalusite 54
Chinese writing rock 55
chlorastrolite 55
chrysanthemum stone 56
chrysoberyl 56
chrysoberyl—cat's-eye 56
chrysocolla 57
chrysoprase—green 57
chrysoprase—lemon 58
cinnabar quartz 58
cinnabar wood 58
citrine—heat-created 59
citrine—natural 59
citrine—rutilated 60
cobalt aura crystal 60
cobaltite 61
copper 61
coral—bamboo 61
coral—black 62
coral—blue 62
coral—Indonesian flower 63
coral—pink 63
coral—red Pacific 63
coral—sponge 64
coral—Tampa Bay (agate fossilized) 64
coral—white 65
covelite 65
creedite 65
crocoite 66
cuprite 66

D

danburite 67
danburite—aqua aura 67
datolite—clear 68

datolite—green 68
diamond 69
dianite 69
diaspor 70
dinosaur bone 70
diopside 70
dioptase 71
dioptase-malachite 71
dolomite—orange 72
dolomite—pink 72
dumortierite—blue 72
dumortierite—purple 73

E

eilat stone 73
emerald 74
epidote 74
erythrite 75
euclase 75
eudialyte 76

F

feldspar 76
flint (chert) 77
fluorite—aqua 77
fluorite—blue 77
fluorite—clear 78
fluorite—green 78
fluorite—pink 79
fluorite—purple 79
fluorite—raspberry 80
fluorite—yellow 80
fossil 81
fossil—ammonite 81
fossil—goniatite 82
fossil—orthoceras 82
fossil—rhyncholampas (echinoids) 82
fossil—turritella 83
freshwater pearl 83
fuchsite 83
fuchsite with kyanite 84
fulgerite 84

G

Gaia stone 85
galena (fool's gold) 85
garnet—golden 85
garnet—green (demantoid) 86
garnet—orange 86
garnet—raspberry 87
garnet—red 87
garnet—yellow-green (grossularite) 88
gaspaite 88
gel lithium silica 88
gem silica 89
goethite 89

gold 90
goldstone—blue 90
goldstone—red 90
goshenite (clear beryl) 91

H
halite (salt)—blue 91
halite (salt)—clear 92
halite (salt)—pink 92
hanksite 93
hawk's eye 93
healers' gold 94
hemalyke 94
hematite 94
hematite—magnetic 94
hemimorphite—aqua 95
hemimorphite—white 95
herderite 96
Herkimer diamond 96
heulandite 97
hiddenite (green kunzite) 97
hole-y stone 98
howlite 98

I
idocrase 98
Indian paint stone 99
indicolite 99
iolite (water sapphire) 99
itacolumite (flexible sandstone) 99
ivory (bone) 100

J
jade—African 100
jade—black 100
jade—green (true jade) 101
jade—lemurian 101
jade—Malaysia 102
jade—mountain 102
jade—pink 102
jade—purple 103
jade—white 103
jade—yellow 104
jasper—bloodstone 104
jasper—brown 104
jasper—bulico 105
jasper—cobra 105
jasper—crazy lace 106
jasper—Dalmatian 106
jasper—fancy 106
jasper—flower 106
jasper—fossil 107
jasper—golden lace 107
jasper—green 108
jasper—Indio 108
jasper—kambaba 109
jasper—leopard skin 109

jasper—mookite 110
jasper—mountain blue 110
jasper—ocean 111
jasper—ocean wave 111
jasper—picture 111
jasper—poppy 112
jasper—rainforest 112
jasper—red 113
jasper—red-banded 113
jasper—royal imperial 114
jasper—silver leaf 114
jasper—snakeskin 114
jasper—spiderweb 115
jasper—stefoinite 115
jasper—yellow 116
jet 116

K

kammerite 116
kinoite 117
kornerupine 117
kunzite—blue 118
kunzite—clear 118
kunzite—green 119
kunzite—pink 119
kunzite—purple 119
kyanite—aqua 120
kyanite—black 120
kyanite—blue 121
kyanite—brown 121
kyanite with rubellite 122

L

labradorite—blue 122
labradorite—golden 123
labradorite—grey 123
labradorite—white 124
Lake Michigan concretion 124
lapis lazuli 124
larimar 125
larvikite 125
lazulite 126
lepidolite 126
lepidolite with mica 127
lepidolite—yellow 127
limonite 127
lodestone 128

M

magnetite 128
malachite 129
malachite—druzy 129
malachite—red 130
malachite stalactites 130
marcasite 130
mariposite 130
meteorite 131
mica 131

mica—muscovite 132
microlite 132
moldavite 132
mookite 133
moonstone—blue 133
moonstone—grey 134
moonstone—peach 134
moonstone—rainbow 135
moonstone—white 135
Moqui marbles 136
morganite (pink beryl) 136
mother-of-pearl—black 136
mother-of-pearl—blister pearl 137
mother-of-pearl—natural 137
mother-of-pearl—white 138
mugglestone (hematite and jasper) 138

N

natrolite 138
neptunite 139
nuumite 139

O

obsidian—aqua 140
obsidian—black 140
obsidian—blue 141
obsidian—cobalt blue 141
obsidian—green 142
obsidian—mahogany 142
obsidian—purple sheen 143
obsidian—rainbow 143
obsidian—red 144
obsidian—snowflake 144
obsidian—vitrophyre 145
okenite 145
onyx—black 146
onyx—blue 146
onyx—green 147
onyx—Mexican white 147
onyx—pha sapha (Black Hills) 147
opal—blue 148
opal—boulder 148
opal—Mexican fire 149
opal—Oregon 149
opal—Owyhee blue 149
opal—white 150
opal aura crystal 150
orpiment—orange 151
orpiment—yellow 151

P

paint stone 152
peacock ore 152
pearl 153
Pecos diamond 153

pectolite 153
peridot 154
Peruvian opal 154
petalite—clear 154
petalite—pink 155
Petoskey stone 155
petrified wood 156
phenacite—white 156
phenacite—yellow 157
Picasso stone 157
picture sandstone 157
pietersite—black 158
pietersite—blue 158
pietersite—brown 159
pietersite—gold 159
pietersite—red 159
pipestone 160
prasiolite 160
prehnite 161
psilomelane 161
pumice 162
purpurite 162
pyrite 162
pyrite with magnetite 163
pyromorphite 163

Q

quartz—black 163
quartz—blue 164
quartz—cactus 164
quartz—candle 164
quartz—cherry 165
quartz—chlorite inclusion 165
quartz—cinnabar 165
quartz—clear crystal 166
quartz—crystal ball 166
quartz—crystal skull 167
quartz—druzy 168
quartz—elestial or skeletal 168
quartz—faden 168
quartz—fairy 169
quartz—fire (lepidochrosite inclusion) 169
quartz—flower of life 169
quartz—fluorite inclusion 170
quartz—girasol 170
quartz—green (prase) 171
quartz—grey phantom 171
quartz—lordite inclusion 172
quartz—Moroccan druzy 172
quartz—Pecos 173
quartz—purple druzy 173
quartz—red 173
quartz—red hair 174
quartz—red phantom 174
quartz—rose 175
quartz—rutilated 175
quartz—scepter 176

quartz—seer stone 176
quartz—smoky 176
quartz—smoky (rutilated) 177
quartz—snow 177
quartz—spirit (amethyst) 178
quartz—spirit (citrine) 178
quartz—spirit (red-violet) 179
quartz—strawberry 179
quartz—tangerine 180
quartz—tourmaline 180
quartz—vogel crystal 180
quartz—white phantom 181

R

rainbow aura crystal 182
rainbow calsilica 182
rhodochrosite 183
rhodochrosite—
gem crystalline 183
rhodonite 183
rhyolite 184
rosasite 184
rose aura crystal 184
rubellite 185
ruby 185
ruby—star 186
ruby with black zoisite 186
ruby with fuchsite 186
ruby with zoisite 187

S

saganite 188
salmonite 188
sapphire—black 188
sapphire—blue 189
sapphire—natural star 190
sapphire—orange (jacinth) 190
sapphire—pink 191
sapphire—purple 191
sapphire—yellow 192
scapolite—gold 192
schorl 193
scolecite 193
sea glass 193
selenite—angel wing 194
selenite—clear 194
selenite—desert rose 195
selenite—green 195
selenite—hour glass 196
selenite—phantom 196
septarian—brown 197
septarian—yellow 197
seraphanite 198
serpentine 198
serpentine jade 198
serpentine jade—olivine 199
shaman stone 199
shattuckite 199
Shiva lingam 200

Siberian quartz—blue 201
Siberian quartz—citrine 201
Siberian quartz—clear 202
Siberian quartz—green 203
Siberian quartz—purple 203
siberite 204
silicified saltstone 204
silver aura crystal 204
smithsonite—aqua 205
smithsonite—pink 205
soapstone 206
sodalite 206
sphalerite 206
spinel—red 207
sponge—fossilized 207
staurolite (fairy cross) 208
stichtite 208
stilbite—orange 208
stilbite—pink 209
stromatolite 209
sugilite 210
sulfur 211
sunstone—orange 211
sunstone—yellow 211

T

tanzanite 212
tektite 212
tempest stone 213
thulite 213
thunder egg 213
tiger eye—black or blue 213
tiger eye—golden 214
tiger eye—red 214
tiger iron (tiger eye with hematite) 214
tinguaite 215
topaz—blue 216
topaz—champagne 216
topaz—clear or white 216
topaz—golden 217
tourmaline—black 217
tourmaline—black velvet 218
tourmaline—blue 218
tourmaline—clear or colorless 219
tourmaline—green 220
tourmaline—pink 220
tourmaline—violet 221
tourmaline—watermelon 221
tremolite 222
tsavorite 222
turquoise—African 222
turquoise—blue 223
turquoise—green 223
turquoise—yellow 224
turritella 224

U
ulexite (TV stone) 224
unakite 225
ussingite 225

V
vanadinite 225
variscite 226
verdelite 226
verdite 226
vesuvianite—green 227
vesuvianite—pink 227
vesuvianite—purple 228
vivianite 228
volcanic glass 228

W
wavellite 229
wonderstone 229
wulfenite 229

Z
zebra stone 230
zincite—clear 230
zincite—green 231
zincite—orange 23
zincite—red 232
zincite—yellow 232
zircon—clear 233
zoisite 233

About *the* Author

A healer for more than twenty-five years, DIANE STEIN is the best-selling author of *Essential Reiki* and more than twenty other books in the fields of metaphysics, women's spirituality, and alternative healing. She lives and teaches in Florida.

Other books by Diane Stein

ESSENTIAL REIKI

A Complete Guide to an Ancient Healing Art

Healer and teacher Diane Stein demystifies the ancient healing practice and makes Reiki techniques available to all in this classic guide.

paperback
8 x 10, 158 pages
ISBN: 978-1-89594-736-9

ESSENTIAL REIKI TEACHING MANUAL

A Companion Guide for Reiki Healers
paperback, 8 x 10, 160 pages
ISBN: 978-1-58091-181-8

DIANE STEIN'S ESSENTIAL REIKI WORKSHOP DVD

2 disks, 254 minutes running time
ISBN: 978-1-58091-180-1

OTHER BOOKS
by DIANE STEIN

ALL WOMEN ARE HEALERS
A Comprehensive Guide to Natural Healing
paperback, 6 x 9, 292 pages
ISBN: 978-1-89594-409-2

CASTING THE CIRCLE
A Woman's Book of Ritual
paperback, 6 x 9, 264 pages
ISBN: 978-1-89594-411-5